MUSICIANS INSTITUTE
™

MASTER CLASS

POP KEYBOARD CONCEPTS

by CHRISTIAN KLIKOVITS

T006242

Now including PLAYBACK+, *a multi-functional audio player that allows you to slow down audio without changing pitch, set loop points, change keys, and pan left or right — available exclusively from Hal Leonard.*

PLAYBACK+
Speed • Pitch • Balance • Loop

To access audio visit:
www.halleonard.com/mylibrary

Enter Code
1350-6322-4891-4951

ISBN 978-1-4950-1929-6

HAL•LEONARD®
CORPORATION
7777 W. BLUEMOUND RD. P.O. BOX 13819 MILWAUKEE, WI 53213

In Australia Contact:
Hal Leonard Australia Pty. Ltd.
4 Lentara Court
Cheltenham, Victoria, 3192 Australia
Email: ausadmin@halleonard.com.au

Visit Hal Leonard Online at
www.halleonard.com

Contents

Introduction

Welcome to *Pop Keyboard Concepts*. For the purpose of this course, I am using the term "pop music" in the larger sense of popular music, and not in the more narrow sense of a subgenre within popular music (as in the *Billboard* pop charts, for example). The material presented here can be found in pop, rock, R&B, funk, soul, folk, and pretty much any other genre of popular music you can name.

As pop keyboard players, we have to wear many different hats. We have to play piano, obviously, but we're also expected to have a certain proficiency in playing electro-mechanical instruments such as electric piano, Hammond organ, or clavinet. (These days, you will frequently play sampled versions of these instruments on digital keyboards or synthesizers.) Often, we have to cover non-keyboard instrument parts in live situations, especially strings and brass. Finally, you should know your way around standard electronic sounds like synth lead, synth bass, and pads. It's beyond the scope of this book to get into the technology side of things; keep in mind that being a well-rounded keyboardist involves more than playing the piano. (Likewise, pushing buttons on a synthesizer or computer is not enough, either; you should be able to get some music out of an acoustic piano.)

The majority of the material presented here applies no matter which keyboard instrument you're playing. Melody, harmony, and rhythm are universal. In many ways, they transcend instrument, style, and time period. While a Mozart piano sonata and a hard rock song sound spectacularly different on the surface, most of those differences are cosmetic. If you go two or three layers deep, you'll find both styles of music are cooking with the same ingredients. (Admittedly, Mozart's dish is rather more complex and sophisticated than the hard rock one.)

All music strikes a balance between composition and improvisation. Classical music tilts heavily toward composition, although there is an element of improvisation as well. (Not everyone plays a piano sonata at the same tempo or with the same dynamics.) Jazz tilts heavily toward improvisation. Most jazz music does have a compositional element, which is then used as the starting point for improvisational exploration – which, for most jazz musicians, is the more important element. Pop music lies somewhere in the middle, between classical and jazz. While there are a lot of keyboard parts that are an integral part of a pop song and have to be played the same way every time you perform the song, there is also a lot of room for improvisation, from creating comping patterns, to interpreting chord charts, to soloing over a chord progression. All of those require a thorough understanding of both music theory and the stylistic conventions of pop music. While this is not a theory book, I will touch on some aspects of it because they provide the necessary context for the practical examples presented.

This book is divided into five parts. In Part One, I present the foundational elements that all Western tonal music (and therefore popular music) is built on: major and minor scales, major and minor triads, intervals. If you already are an intermediate or advanced player, this material may be familiar to you. However, before you skip ahead to the more advanced sections of the book, make sure you know all these scales and chords inside out, in every key. Did I mention you have to be able to play in every key? Yes, even F♯.

Parts Two, Three, and Four each explore in detail one of the main aspects of music: the horizontal aspect, which we call **melody**; the vertical aspect, which we call **harmony**; and the temporal aspect, which we call **rhythm**. There is obviously a lot of overlap between these three aspects in music. (Most of what we play has a melodic, harmonic, and rhythmic element.) For the sake of study, though, it is often helpful to isolate certain concepts and look at them individually.

Finally, in Part Five I present detailed analyses of a number of examples of accompaniment parts and keyboard solos. These examples demonstrate how the material presented in the first four parts plays out in music you might encounter in real-world situations.

–Christian Klikovits

Part One
The Basics

In this first part of the course, we'll look at the most important melodic and harmonic elements of virtually all Western music: major and natural minor scales, and major and minor triads. Everything else is an extension, or derivative, or variation, or elaboration of these basic concepts. For example, if I am thoroughly familiar with the concept of a major triad, it is easy to understand an augmented triad as a major triad with a raised fifth, or to understand a major seventh chord as a major triad with another note added on top.

Analogously, if I am thoroughly familiar with the concept of a natural minor scale, it is easy to understand a harmonic minor scale as a natural minor scale with a raised seventh scale degree.

Chapter 1 presents the first five notes of each major and minor scale and the major and minor triads created by the first, third, and fifth notes of these scales, as well as the intervals that can be derived from those five notes. For beginners, it is a good idea to learn these five-note scales first, because you don't have to worry about passing the thumb. Putting your right-hand thumb on the note C, the second finger on D, third finger on E, fourth finger on F, and fifth finger on G gives you a five-note hand position that encompasses five of the seven notes of a major or minor scale, as well as the three notes of the triad.

Note: In piano playing, the fingers get assigned numbers for the purpose of specifying fingering, starting on the thumb of each hand, so the thumb is always the first finger, the index finger is the second finger, and so on.

In **Chapter 2**, we'll add the remaining two notes to form complete major and natural minor scales. These should be practiced in all keys, with the correct fingerings.

Chapter 3 presents all the major and minor triads together in one exercise.

Five-Note Scales

1

There are 12 different notes in our musical system, and therefore 12 major scales, 12 minor scales, 12 major triads, and 12 minor triads. Almost everything you'll encounter in popular music can be derived from this basic melodic and harmonic material, by way of various transformations. It is therefore imperative to know these scales and chords inside out, in all 12 keys.

We'll start with the first five notes of each major and minor scale. That way, you can familiarize yourself with most of the notes of the scales without having to pass the thumb. The notes of the tonic triad, the triad built on the root of a key, are included in these five-note scales. We can also derive a number of important intervals from them, namely the major second, the major and minor thirds, the perfect fourth, and the perfect fifth.

Here is the five-note major scale starting on the note C, with the correct fingering for the right hand:

The first, third, and fifth notes of this scale form a C major triad:

Lowering the third note by a half step gives us a C minor scale and a C minor triad:

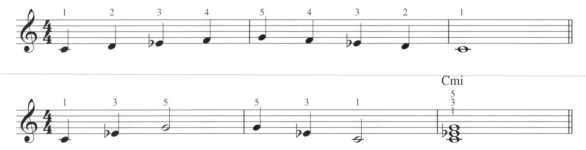

Here are the intervals we can derive from the five-note scale in C major:

Chapter 1

The exercise on the following pages presents these scales and triads in all 12 major and minor keys. Again, they are the foundation for things to come, so make sure you are thoroughly familiar with all of them.

Enharmonic Spelling

Notice that there is a major key exercise starting on the note F♯ and one starting on G♭. These are obviously the same note (this is called "enharmonic" spelling), but since you're equally likely to encounter the key of F♯ or the key of G♭, you should be able to think of this scale either way. The same goes for D♯ minor and E♭ minor. Also, for some notes the major key is a flat key and the minor key is a sharp key (for example, D♭ major and C♯ minor).

The Five-Note Scale in All Major and Minor Keys

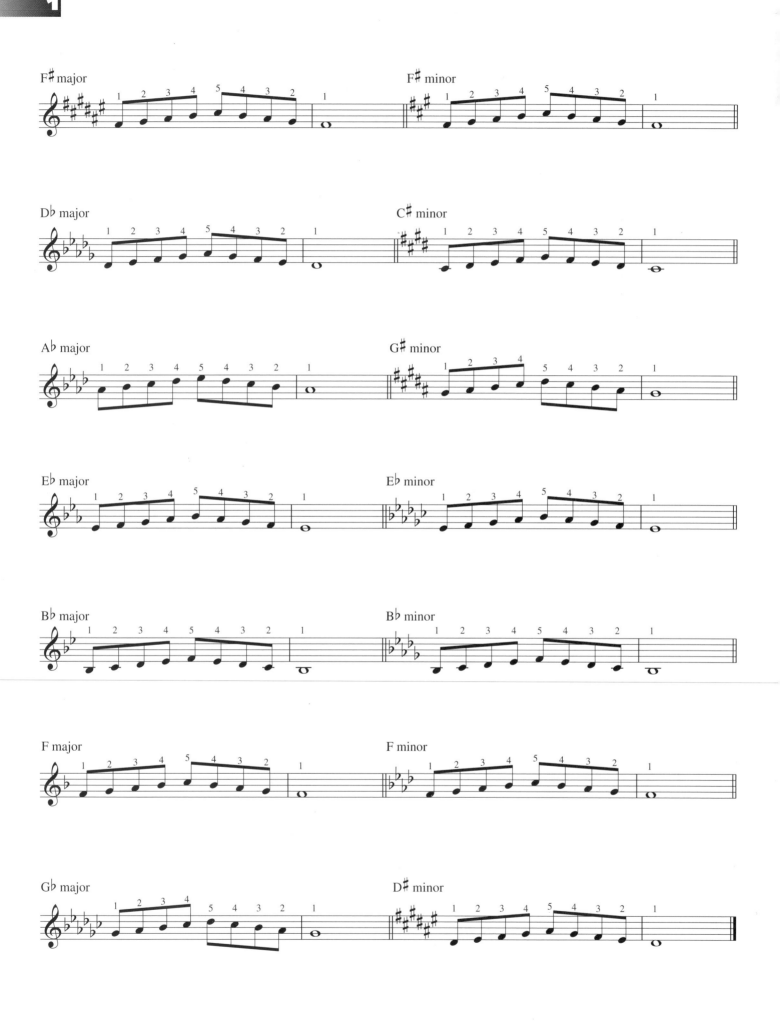

2 Major and Natural Minor Scales

The Major Scale

In this chapter, we will expand from the five-note scales of Chapter 1 to the full seven-note (or "hepta-tonic") scales known as the major scale and the natural minor scale. As mentioned in the introduction, these scales form the melodic framework in which tonal music, and specifically pop music, operates. It is important to be able to move comfortably around these scales on the piano. For a pop keyboardist, it may not be as important to practice scales for hours every day like many classical players do, or to know a wide variety of different scales like jazz players have to, but you do have to know the major and minor scales inside and out, and you do have to know the proper fingering for these scales.

Adding a major sixth interval (from the root of the scale) and a major seventh interval to the five-note major scale of chapter one creates a major scale:

As far as fingering goes, there is a relatively simple system that can be applied to all major and minor scales, with slight variations. What all the scales have in common is that you can divide them into a group of three consecutive notes (played by the first, second, and third fingers), and a group of four consecutive notes (played by the first, second, third, and fourth fingers). The groups in the C major scale are as follows:

The fifth finger is often used when the scale changes direction:

Scales should be practiced over a range of at least two octaves. When playing the C major scale, you just repeat the 1-2-3 and 1-2-3-4 groupings until you want to turn around, at which point you use the fifth finger for the top note:

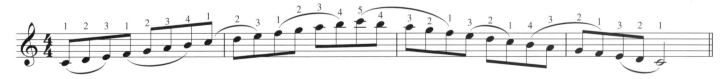

The same fingering works for the D, E, G, A, and B major scales. The F major scale is different in that the group of four notes happens first, followed by the group of three. Other than that, the idea is the same: group of four, group of three, group of four, group of three. When you want to turn around, you use the fourth finger in this case:

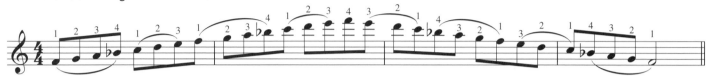

With scales that start on a black key, things get a little more complicated. The grouping still remains, but now the root of the scale does not coincide with the beginning of a group. Here's an easy way to think about the fingerings for the Db, Eb, Ab, and Bb major scales: Play exactly like you would a C major scale (in other words, the group of three starts with the thumb on C, and the group of four starts with the thumb on F), and then just adjust for the flats in the scale. So in the key of Db, the first group is C-Db-Eb instead of C-D-E. The following example shows a comparison of the groupings for the C major scale with those for Db, Eb, Ab, and Bb:

With the final major scale, the one in Gb, there is an extra little twist; here, the C is flat. The basic idea is the same, though: The first group is Cb-Db-Eb, and the second group is F-Gb-Ab-Bb.

The Natural Minor Scale

Adding a minor sixth interval (from the root of the scale) and a minor seventh interval to the five-note minor scale of chapter one creates a natural minor scale:

Comparing the major scale to the natural minor scale, we find that the former contains a major third, sixth, and seventh, and the latter contains a minor third, sixth, and seventh:

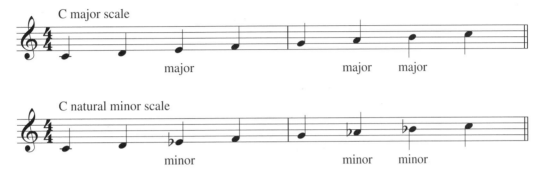

The reason this scale is called natural minor and not just minor is that there are other minor scales, so one has to be specific. More on that later.

As far as fingering, the C, D, E, F, G, A, and B natural minor scales – all the ones that start on a white key – have the same fingering as the major scales starting on the same note. For example, compare the fingering for the D major and D natural minor scales:

Relative Major and Minor Keys

Before we look at the rest of the minor scale fingerings, we have to examine the concept of relative keys. Every major scale shares its key signature with a minor scale whose root is a minor third down (or major sixth up) from the root of the major scale. So the keys of C major and A minor share the same key signature, and therefore the same notes. So do the keys of D major and B minor, G♭ major and E♭ minor, and so on. Compare the relative keys of E major and C♯ minor – both have four sharps in the key signature:

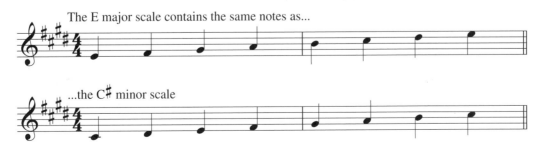

The fingerings for those two scales are identical insofar as the same fingers play on the same notes in both scales. In other words, playing a C# minor scale is the same as playing an E major scale, only starting on C# instead of E:

The same relationship exists between the relative keys of G♭ major and E♭ minor, A major and F♯ minor, B major and G♯ minor, and D♭ major and B♭ minor.

The exercises on the following pages take you through all major and minor scales. Playing the 1, 2, 3, and 1, 2, 3, 4 groupings as note clusters is a good way to get a feel for the geography of a particular scale. On the first scale, C, fingerings are given over a range of two octaves. Apply the same idea to the other scales.

The C Major Scale

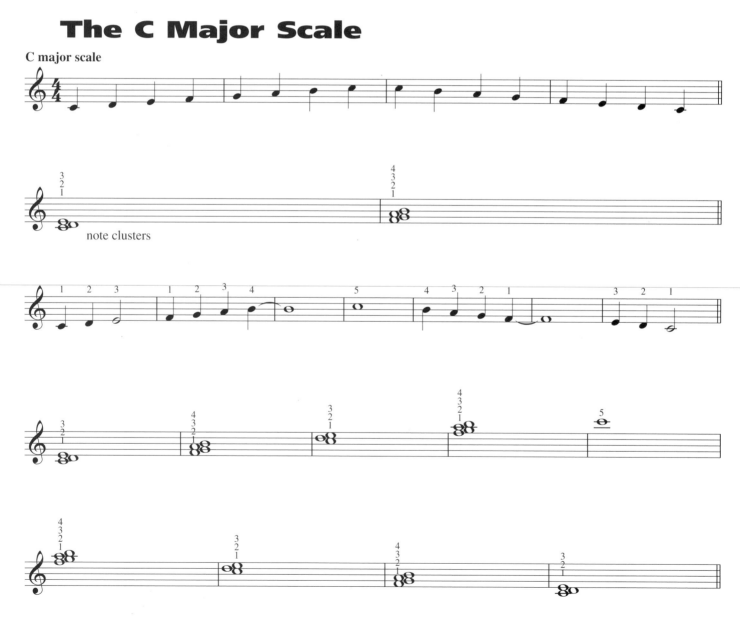

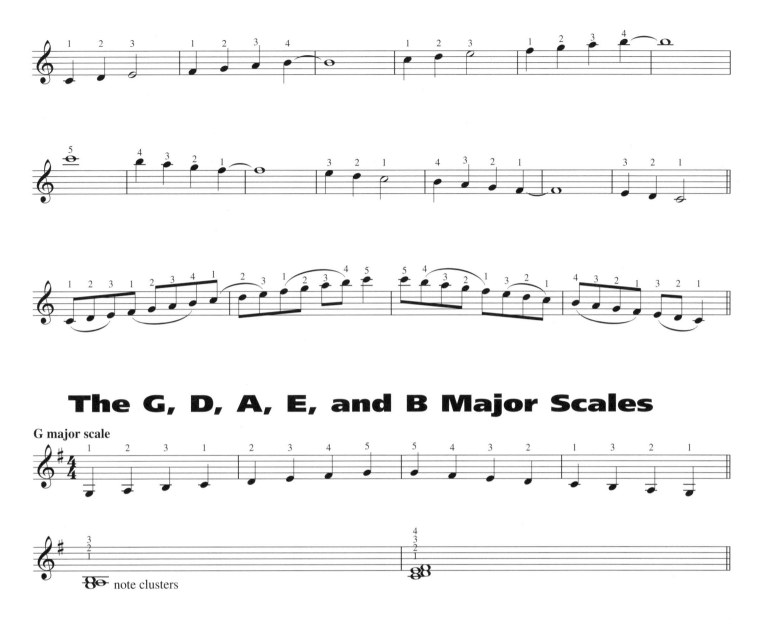

The G, D, A, E, and B Major Scales

G major scale

D major scale

A major scale

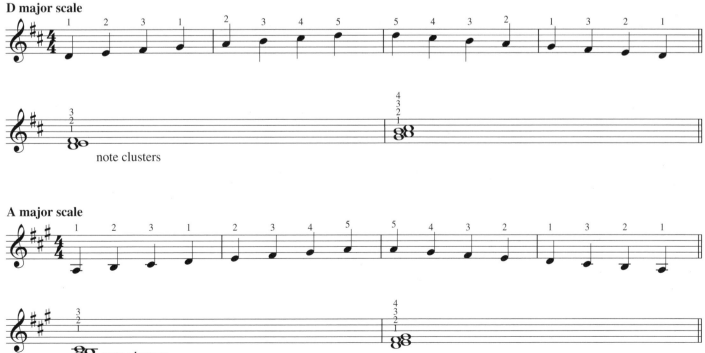

E major scale

B major scale

The D♭, E♭, A♭, And B♭ Major Scales

D♭ major scale

note clusters

root

Eb major scale

note clusters

Ab major scale

note clusters

B♭ major scale

note clusters

The F and G♭ Major Scales

F major scale

note clusters

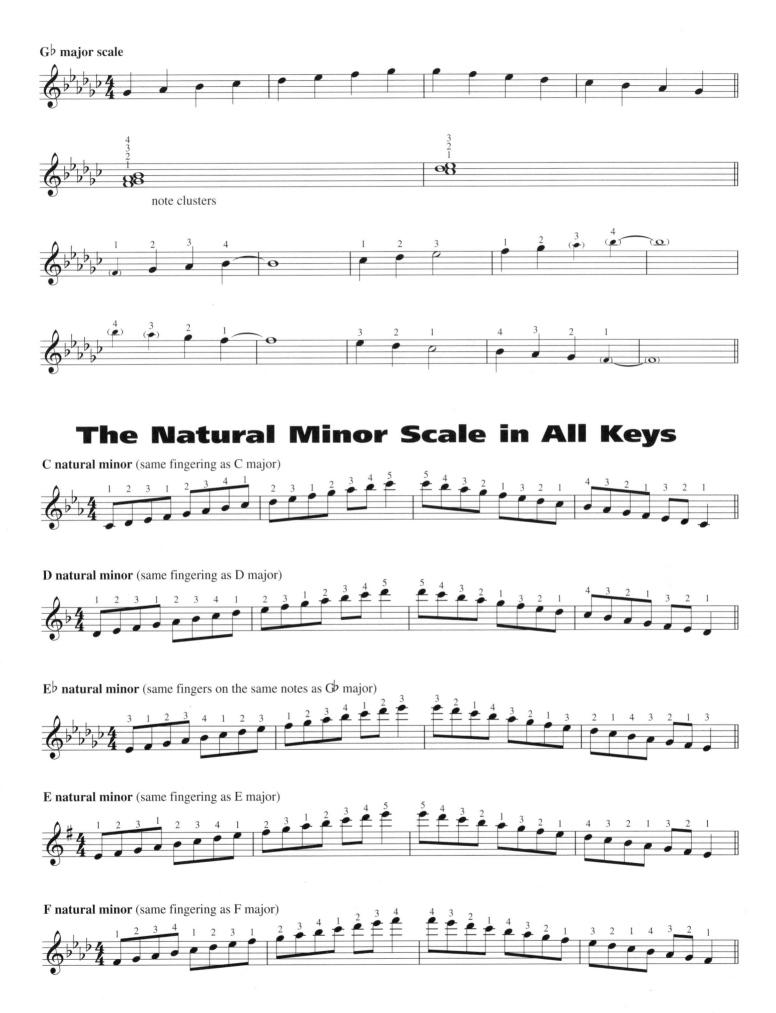

G♭ major scale

note clusters

The Natural Minor Scale in All Keys

C natural minor (same fingering as C major)

D natural minor (same fingering as D major)

E♭ natural minor (same fingers on the same notes as G♭ major)

E natural minor (same fingering as E major)

F natural minor (same fingering as F major)

F♯ natural minor (same fingers on the same notes as A major)

G natural minor (same fingering as G major)

G♯ natural minor (same fingers on the same notes as B major)

A natural minor (same fingering as A major)

B♭ natural minor (same fingers on the same notes as D♭ major)

B natural minor (same fingering as B major)

C♯ natural minor (same fingers on the same notes as E major)

Triads

3

As we've seen, we can derive major and minor triads from major and minor scales by playing the first, third, and fifth notes of the respective scale. These chord structures are the foundation of the harmonic language of popular music – and most other music, for that matter. While there are many different chords that can be created by altering or adding notes, the basic major and minor triads are the most common and important ones. You need to be proficient in playing these chords in all keys.

The exercise in this chapter shows major and minor triads in all keys. Again, notice that some chords are presented with different enharmonic spellings, like D♭ minor and C♯ minor. (They contain the same notes, but are spelled differently.) In some cases, this leads to chords with double flats or double sharps, which is not for the faint of heart. But because of the extreme importance of these chord structures, you should be able to think of them with either spelling. Remember the following enharmonic equivalents:

- C♯/D♭
- D♯/E♭
- E♯/F
- F♯/G♭

- G♯/A♭
- A♯/B♭
- B/C♭

Major and Minor Triads in All Keys

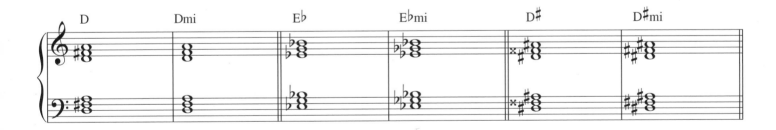

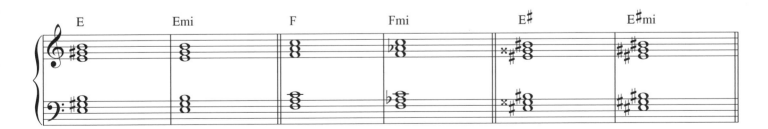

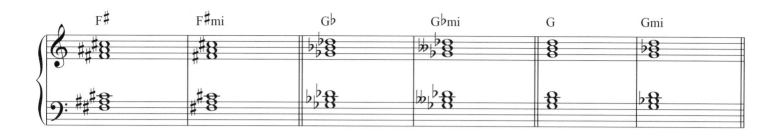

Part Two
Harmony

In Part One, we established the melodic and harmonic foundation of tonal music. Now, in Part Two, we'll look at how the basic harmonic vocabulary of major and minor triads can be expanded in various ways to form the rich harmonic language of popular music.

When it comes to harmony, there are three main aspects:

- **Chord structure:** What intervals comprise a chord? How do you voice it on the keyboard?

- **Chord function:** What function does a chord have relative to the key the piece is in?

- **Chord progression:** How are chords put together into progressions?

In **Chapter 4**, we'll examine different ways of voicing the triads we already know.

Chapter 5 presents the other chord structures you're likely to find in pop music.

Chapter 6 deals with the function of chords within the diatonic system.

In **Chapter 7**, we'll look at chord progression, the movement from harmony to harmony.

In principle, you can use any type of chord in any style of music. However, there are certain general tendencies you should be aware of. In jazz music, you'll find seventh and extended chords almost exclusively. R&B also uses a lot of seventh chords, in addition to triads. In pop music (the subgenre), you'll find every type of chord, although simple triads are much more common here than in other styles. In rock, you'll find a lot of power chords. Hard rock and metal use power chords predominantly.

As a general rule, songs use either mostly triads or mostly seventh and extended chords. You should not mix chords randomly from different categories. That does not mean you can't do it, but there should be a good reason for it. "I just learned about major-seventh-sharp-eleventh (maj7$\sharp$11) chords, so let me throw a couple of them into this country song I'm playing" is not the right approach. You should use a particular chord because it sounds right and fits with the chords around it.

Every chord structure has a particular quality to it, a distinct sound you need to be familiar with. Sounds evoke feelings. Play any chord; let it ring out. Observe how it makes you feel, and how the vibration in the room is affected. Play a C major triad and let it ring for a while, and then play a C minor triad. Listen deeply and notice how this change affects you. Remember, improvising or composing music means to choose colors, and you have to be familiar with the available colors to use them well.

Analogously, the frequency with which certain chord progressions or chord functions are used is a big part of what distinguishes one style of music from another, and you should be aware of those distinctions.

Working with Triads

4

There are a few transformations that can be applied to the basic triads from Part One: inversions, doubled notes, and open-position voicings.

Inversions

There are three different ways to play a basic three-note triad. The one we've been using so far is called **root position**. It has the root of the chord (the note that gives the chord its name) at the bottom. In the case of a C major triad, that would be – in ascending order – C, E, and G.

If you take the lowest note, C, and move it up an octave, you get what is called a different **inversion** of that same chord. It is called a first-inversion chord. In the case of C major, it would be E, G, and C.

Moving the lowest note up an octave again results in a second-inversion chord. In the case of C major, it would be G, C, and E.

Which one of these to choose depends on several factors, including voice leading (the rules governing the movement of the notes of one chord to the notes of the next one – more on that later), range, melody (if you're using a chord to harmonize a melody note), and personal preference. In certain situations, first- or second-inversion triads sound better than their root-position counterparts. Most of the time, voice leading will be the deciding factor.

You should be comfortable with playing chords in any inversion, not just root position – although the latter is usually the easiest to find on the keyboard, because that is how we learn chord structures in the first place. This applies to all chord types, but it is especially crucial when it comes to triads.

Doubled Notes

Triads are often played as a four-note chord, with one doubled note. This adds weight and volume. It also makes the top note sound more like a melody note, since that note is doubled and therefore reinforced at the bottom of the voicing; that is helpful if you're harmonizing a melody. Generally, the lowest note determines the inversion, so the chord C-E-G-C is in root position.

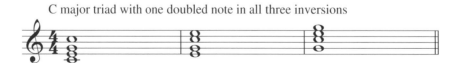

If you distribute the notes of a triad between both hands, more than one note can be doubled, and some notes can even be tripled or quadrupled.

Chapter 4

Note: A distinction has to be made between chord and voicing. A chord is a certain combination of distinct pitches. For example, the pitches C, E, and G constitute a C major triad, no matter how you scramble them or how many notes you double. A voicing, on the other hand, is a specific way of playing that chord – for example, a different order of the notes constitutes a different voicing, as shown here.

Open Position versus Close Position

We need to be aware of the important distinction between open-position and close-position voicings. In close position, you can't fit a chord tone between any two notes of the voicings. In other words, all the pitches are as close together as possible. Anything other than that constitutes an open-position voicing.

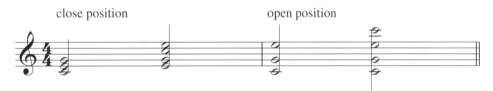

Both open- and close-position voicings sound great, but close position is more common in keyboard playing. That's because those voicings are easy to play with one hand, freeing the other hand to play a melody, or a bass line, whereas most open-position voicings require two hands.

Practice the following exercise to familiarize yourself with triad inversions, and then transpose it to all 12 keys.

Triads with Inversions

(to be practiced in all 12 keys)

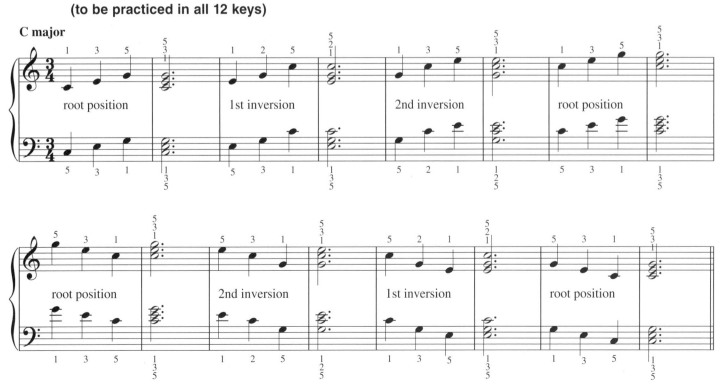

C minor

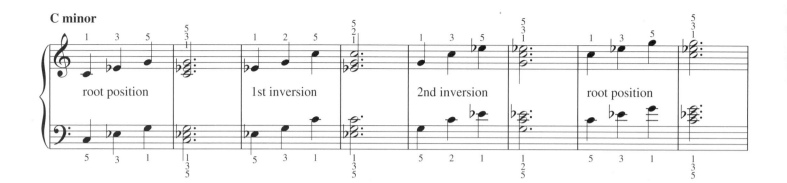

root position   1st inversion   2nd inversion   root position

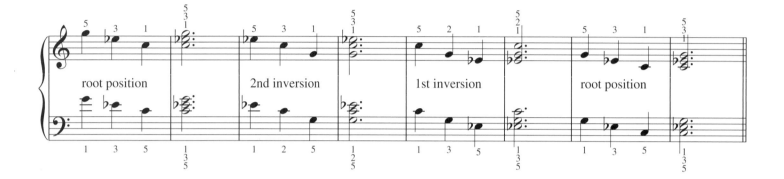

root position   2nd inversion   1st inversion   root position

Chord Types

5

So far, our harmonic vocabulary consists of major triads and minor triads, the two most frequent chords in popular music. This chapter introduces the other harmonic structures found in pop songs. These chords can be categorized into several groups:

- **Triads with one note changed or left out:** augmented triads, diminished triads, suspended chords, power chords

- **Triads with added notes:** add9 chords, sixth chords, 6/9 chords

- **Seventh chords:** a whole new set of (four-note) chords created by adding the interval of a seventh (from the root) to a major, minor, augmented, or diminished triad

- **Extended chords:** variations of seventh chords created by adding ninth and/or eleventh and/or thirteenth intervals to a seventh chord

- **Slash chords:** harmonic structures created by superimposing a chord (most often a triad) over an individual bass note

Along with the chords themselves, we will study the correct **chord symbols**, the shorthand used in sheet music and on chord charts to express harmonic structures and progressions.

Chord symbols are one the most important elements of contemporary music notation. Although commonly associated with popular music, musicians in the Baroque period already used a system called "figured bass," which was essentially a system of chord symbols. Chord nomenclature is not an exact science. There are certain things that most everybody agrees on, and then there are things that are heavily disputed. The conventions presented in this course are the results of many years of personal experience of someone who writes and reads charts on a daily basis. While there are always a few things that come down to personal preference, most professional musicians will agree with most of what is presented here.

Interpreting chord symbols is an integral part of a musician's job. Unlike classical music, where every pitch is notated (for the most part), popular music depends to a large extent on a player's skill in creating parts themselves, based on the chord progression and the style of the song.

Before we get into the new chord types, let's look at the correct chord symbols for major and minor triads. The chord symbol for a major triad is the letter name by itself. Avoid using a suffix for this chord; it is redundant, and can be confused with other chord qualities.

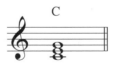

The best symbol for a minor triad is the suffix "mi" after the letter name. Avoid using a minus sign (−) to denote minor triads. The suffixes "m" and "min" are not wrong, but "mi" is preferable.

Triads with One Note Changed or Left Out

The Augmented Triad

An augmented triad consists of a root, major third, and augmented fifth, and can be thought of as a major triad with the fifth raised a half step. It is highly unstable, and is almost always resolved. Its dissonant quality lies in the fact that it is not derived from any diatonic major or minor scale. (It does occur in the harmonized melodic minor and harmonic minor scales, but not in the natural minor scale.) It is relatively rare in pop music, and is generally used as a passing chord. The usual chord symbols used are the suffix "aug" and the plus sign (+). The plus sign is preferable; it should always be used to denote a raised fifth, even in the context of larger chords. Here's a C augmented triad with the correct chord symbol, and a couple of typical chord progressions containing an augmented triad:

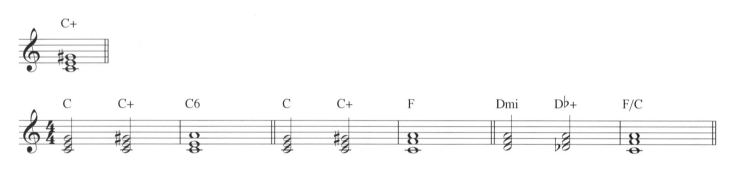

The Diminished Triad

A diminished triad consists of a root, minor third, and diminished fifth, and can be thought of as a minor triad with the fifth lowered a half step. It is also unstable and exhibits a strong tendency toward resolution. It contains a tritone interval between the root and the diminished fifth; tritones always strive toward resolution. In its pure form, this chord is relatively rare in pop music, although it occurs occasionally. The symbols commonly used are a little circle, or the suffix "dim." Both are okay to use; I prefer the circle.

The Sus4 Chord

A sus4 chord consists of a root, perfect fourth, and perfect fifth, and can be thought of as a major triad with the third raised a half step. "Sus" is short for suspended. It means that the third is replaced by another note, either the fourth or the second. The sus4 chord is somewhat more common than the sus2 chord. Suspended chords are ubiquitous in popular music.

Suspended chords developed in the classical tradition, and for a long time they absolutely had to be resolved. Here's the typical resolution of a sus4 chord:

As music evolved and people's tolerance for dissonance grew, composers started using suspended chords as legitimate chord structures that didn't necessarily have to be resolved. They are often used for the purpose of harmonic obfuscation. Harmonic obfuscation refers to the practice of rendering chord progressions ambiguous in order to create interest. Suspensions, slash chords, and power chords are the main tools to achieve this.

If the chord symbol only says "sus," it is understood that the fourth replaces the third. Sus4 in the chord symbol is also acceptable.

The Sus2 Chord

A sus2 chord consists of a root, major second, and perfect fifth. The second is played in place of the third. Refer to the remarks about sus4 chords; the same applies to sus2 chords. The chord symbol 5/2 is sometimes used for this chord, but sus2 is preferable because it illustrates the fact that this chord is a variation of a regular triad whereby the third is replaced with another note, just like the sus4 chord.

Suspended chords are often used in a technique called "elaboration of static harmony." It is a way to create movement in the context of a basically static chord (for example, C-Csus4-C).

The Power Chord

A power chord consists of a root and a perfect fifth. It is a dyad, a chord made up of two notes. The proper chord symbol is the letter name followed by the number 5. Below are two familiar ways of voicing a power chord:

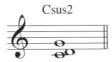

Power chords are an integral part of popular music, especially rock. The lack of a third gives them an open, somewhat ambiguous quality. Power chords don't commit to a major or minor tonality, although oftentimes the context will suggest a key. In the example below, the guitar part contains only power chords, but the melody fills in the missing thirds, thereby clarifying the chord progression.

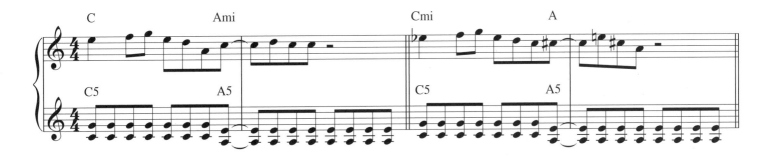

Triads with Added Notes

The next group of chords consists of major or minor triads that have an added major sixth, an added major ninth, or both an added major sixth and major ninth. Chords with an added sixth or both an added sixth and added ninth occur occasionally in pop music, and all the time in jazz. With add9 chords it's the other way around: They occur occasionally in jazz, and they're ubiquitous in pop music.

The Major Add9 Chord

A major add9 chord consists of a root, major third, perfect fifth, and major ninth. This chord is an everyday feature in popular music. Adding the ninth is a great way to fatten up a major triad without changing the basic chord quality.

This is one of the most heavily contended chords in the context of chord nomenclature. Many people use the number 2 (which I don't recommend), or add2 to denote this chord. I prefer "(add 9)" because it is difficult to confuse with anything else. C(add9) means exactly that: a major triad with an added ninth. You will see this chord symbol with or without parentheses; both are okay to use.

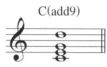

In terms of voicing, it does not matter whether you add the ninth in the middle of the voicing or on top of it. Here are several common voicings for this chord:

The Minor Add9 Chord

A minor add9 chord consists of a root, minor third, perfect fifth, and major ninth. The remarks about the major add9 chord also apply to the minor add9 chord.

Here are several common voicings for a minor add9 chord:

The Major Sixth Chord

A major sixth chord consists of a root, major third, perfect fifth, and major sixth. Here is a C major sixth chord with the correct chord symbol:

The Minor Sixth Chord

A minor sixth chord consists of a root, minor third, perfect fifth, and major sixth. Here is a C minor sixth chord with the correct chord symbol:

The Major 6/9 Chord

A major 6/9 chord consists of a root, major third, perfect fifth, major sixth, and major ninth. Here is a C major 6/9 chord with the correct chord symbol:

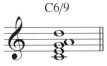

The Minor 6/9 Chord

A minor 6/9 chord consists of a root, minor third, perfect fifth, major sixth, and major ninth. Here is a C minor 6/9 chord with the correct chord symbol:

Seventh Chords

Seventh chords are created by adding the interval of a seventh (from the tonic) to a triad. The quality of the seventh can be major, minor, or diminished. The most important seventh chords are major seventh, dominant seventh, minor seventh, and minor seventh flat five (mi7♭5). In addition, there are a few less frequent seventh chords you should be familiar with.

Seventh chords are used quite a bit in pop music, although not as often as triads, power chords, and add9 chords.

The Major Seventh Chord

A major seventh chord consists of a root, major third, perfect fifth, and major seventh. Here is a C major seventh chord with the correct chord symbol:

The Dominant Seventh Chord

A dominant seventh chord consists of a root, major third, perfect fifth, and minor seventh. Here is a C dominant seventh chord with the correct chord symbol:

The Minor Seventh Chord

A minor seventh chord consists of a root, minor third, perfect fifth, and minor seventh. Here is a C minor seventh chord with the correct chord symbol:

The Minor Seventh Flat Five Chord

A minor seventh flat five chord consists of a root, minor third, diminished fifth, and minor seventh. Many people use mi7♭5 as the symbol for this chord, which is perfectly acceptable. I prefer the little circle with the slash through it, because it takes up a lot less space, and it can't be confused with anything else. Sometimes there is a 7 after the slashed circle, which is also acceptable. Here is a C minor seventh flat five chord (Cmi7♭5) with the correct chord symbol:

The Diminished Seventh Chord

A diminished seventh chord consists of a root, minor third, diminished fifth, and diminished seventh. Here is a C diminished seventh chord with the correct chord symbol:

The Minor Major Seventh Chord

A minor major seventh chord consists of a root, minor third, perfect fifth, and major seventh. Here is a C minor major seventh chord with the correct chord symbol:

The Dominant Seventh Sus4 Chord

A dominant seventh sus4 chord consists of a root, perfect fourth, perfect fifth, and minor seventh. As with suspended triads, the suffix "sus" in itself denotes a suspended fourth. Here is a C dominant seventh sus4 chord with the correct chord symbol:

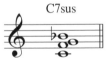

Extended Chords

Extended chords are seventh chords that have been enlarged by adding notes at the top, resulting in ninth, eleventh, and thirteenth chords. The added notes themselves (called "extensions") can be diatonic (also called "natural") or chromatic (also called "altered"). A chord can have more than one extension; it is even possible to combine natural and altered extensions in the same chord (e.g., a natural ninth and an altered eleventh).

Extended chords with more than one added diatonic note are usually named after the highest numbered extension. If a chord has a ninth and an eleventh, for example, it is notated as an eleventh chord. The number of the extension replaces the 7 in the chord symbol. For instance, adding a ninth to a C dominant seventh chord turns the chord symbol from C7 to C9. Be mindful of the fact that the seventh is still understood to be part of the chord; it is just replaced by the ninth in the chord symbol for the sake of brevity.

A C minor eleventh chord is notated as Cmi11. The seventh is understood to be part of the chord. The ninth, however, is optional; whether or not to include it depends on the context, and on personal preference.

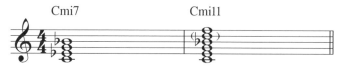

Altered extensions should always be included in the chord symbols. They do not replace the seventh. Adding a minor ninth to a C dominant seventh chord changes the chord symbol from C7 to C7(♭9). The ♭ and ♯ signs are used to denote alterations. Note that natural extensions appear right after the letter name, but altered extensions are always in parentheses. Avoid things like (-9), or (+11). The only alteration that is expressed with a plus sign is a raised fifth: + always means augmented fifth.

Now, let's look at each of the main seventh chords and their possible extensions.

Extended Major Seventh Chords

Major seventh chords can be extended with a major ninth, a major thirteenth, and an augmented eleventh. These extensions can appear by themselves, or in various combinations. Here are the conventional options. (Note that the ninth is optional if higher numbered extensions are present.)

Extended Minor Seventh Chords

Minor seventh chords can be extended with a major ninth, a perfect eleventh, and (less often) a perfect thirteenth.

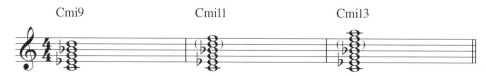

Extended Minor Seventh Flat Five Chords

Minor seventh flat five chords can be extended with a major ninth and a perfect eleventh.

Extended Dominant Seventh Chords

Dominant chords provide by far the most opportunities for both extension and alteration. The ninth can be major, minor, or augmented. The eleventh can only be augmented. The thirteenth can be major or minor. As mentioned before, altered extensions always appear in parentheses. Here are several extended dominant seventh chords:

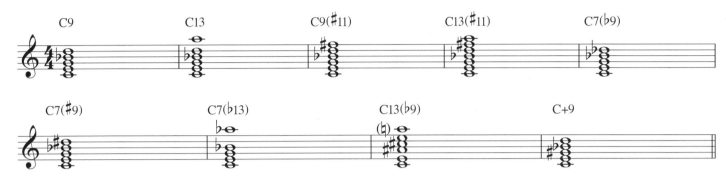

Slash Chords

The last group of new chords is called slash chords. Slash chords consist of two parts: a chord and a bass note, separated by a slash. C/G (pronounced "C over G") means to play a C major triad with a G bass note.

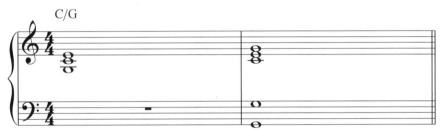

The "chord" part of a slash chord is usually a triad, but it can be any other chord structure, as well.

Slash chords commonly fall into one of three categories: inversions, incomplete extended chords, and random chord/bass note combinations.

Inversions

Slash chord symbols are often used to denote a specific chord inversion. C/G means that whichever instrument plays the bass part should play the fifth of the chord. (This could be a bass, a bassoon, a trombone, or the keyboard player's left hand.) Technically, inversions pertain to the whole arrangement, so if the pianist plays a root-position triad and the bass player plays the third of the chord, then the whole chord is considered to be in first inversion.

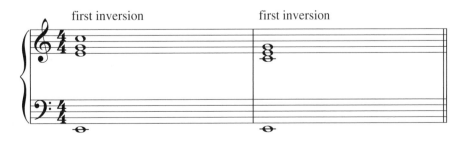

Incomplete Extended Chords

Sometimes slash chords are incomplete extended chords by implication. G/C, for example, could denote a C major ninth chord without a third.

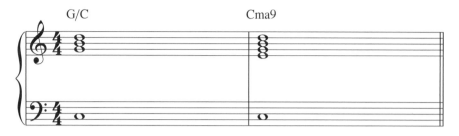

It is standard practice to use slash notation to denote a dominant ninth sus4 chord. This is one of the most important slash chords; it occurs in every style of popular music. Here are three different voicings and chord symbols for what is basically the same chord:

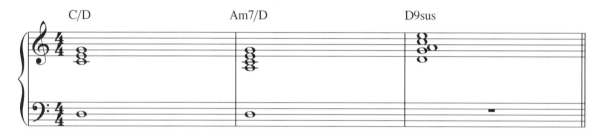

Random Chord/ Bass Note Combinations

In principle, any chord can be played against any bass note. However, a lot of those combinations are so dissonant as to render them unusable in all but the most adventurous of musical contexts. Some of them are useful, though, and slash notation is a convenient way of notating them. Here are several random combinations:

Chord Function

6

A thorough understanding of chord progressions is an integral part of musicianship. Virtually everything in Western music, including chord progressions, is based upon the diatonic system; in other words, major and minor scales.

The chords that form progressions in pop music fall, for the most part, into one of four categories: 1) diatonic chords; 2) modal interchange; 3) secondary dominants; 4) modulation. Diatonic chords are the basic material for progressions, while the other chord categories expand the harmonic palette by introducing various degrees of chromaticism. Let's look at each of these categories.

Diatonic Chords

The word diatonic means "belonging to a particular key or scale." Melodically, it can refer to individual notes or entire melodies; harmonically, it can refer to individual chords or chord progressions. For example, saying that a certain melody is diatonic in the key of C means that it contains only notes occurring in the C major scale. Likewise, a chord that's diatonic in the key of C contains only notes from the C major scale.

"Harmonizing a scale" is an important concept in music. It means building a chord (vertical structure) on each note of a scale (horizontal structure), using only notes from that scale. Here is a C **major scale**, first harmonized with triads and then with basic seventh chords.

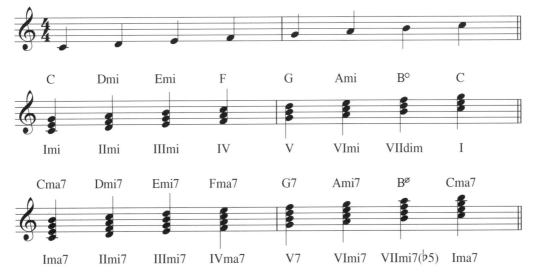

Progressions using any combination of diatonic chords will sound coherent because of the strong sense of tonality created by chords derived from a particular scale. In most pop songs, a large portion of, and often all, the chords you hear will be diatonic.

In minor keys, things get a little more complex. This is because there are three different minor scales: 1) natural minor; 2) harmonic minor; 3) melodic minor.

The **natural minor scale** is the most fundamental form of minor scale. If you write out a scale on a staff with a minor key signature, you get a natural minor scale. It contains the same notes as the relative major scale, albeit starting on a different note.

Here is a C natural minor scale and its relative major scale.

Below is a C natural minor scale, harmonized with triads, and basic seventh chords.

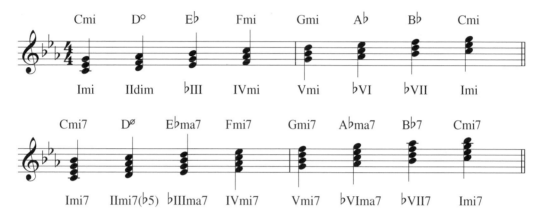

The **harmonic minor scale** was created to remedy a problem presented by the natural minor scale: the lack of a "leading tone." The leading tone is the note a major seventh interval up from the tonic (the root of the key). This note has important melodic and harmonic implications. If I play a diatonic V–I progression in a major key, you can clearly hear the effect of the leading tone. By contrast, if I then play a similar progression using chords from the natural minor scale, you can hear that the resolution is not quite as convincing. This is because the leading tone is missing. The first progression features the major seventh of the key, in this case B♮; the second one uses the minor seventh, in this case B♭.

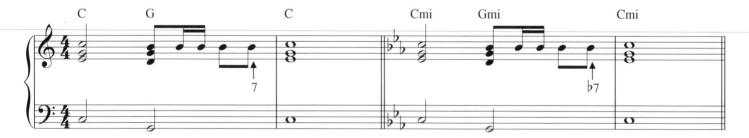

If you look at a harmonic minor scale, you'll notice that the raised seventh scale degree provides the leading tone that was missing in the natural minor scale.

If we harmonize this scale, we now get a major triad or dominant seventh chord on the fifth scale degree. This V chord is more popular than the diatonic V chord derived from the natural minor scale. Here is a harmonic minor scale, harmonized first with triads, and then with basic seventh chords:

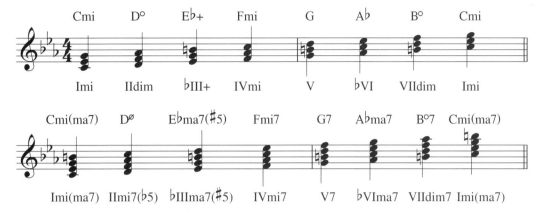

While the raised seventh scale degree in the harmonic minor scale solves the problem of the missing leading tone, it creates a new problem: an augmented second interval between the minor sixth and the major seventh.

augmented second

Melodically, this is not particularly smooth; it gives this scale its characteristic, almost oriental, sound. (This scale works better harmonically than melodically, hence the name "harmonic" minor.) In order to remedy this, the melodic minor scale was invented.

The **melodic minor scale** has both a raised sixth and seventh scale degree. In classical music, a distinction is made between an ascending and a descending melodic minor scale. The descending scale is played like a natural minor scale. In popular music, this distinction is unnecessary. For our purposes, the melodic minor scale has a raised sixth and seventh degree, whether ascending or descending. Below is a C melodic minor scale, harmonized first with triads, and then with basic seventh chords:

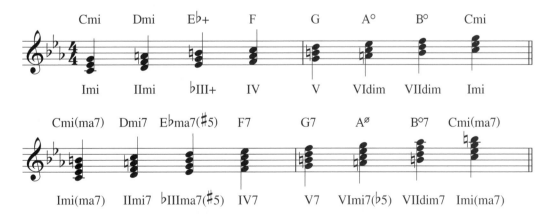

All three minor scales are used in popular music, but progressions predominantly use chords from the natural minor scale, and the V chord from harmonic minor, as mentioned above. The harmonized major, natural minor, harmonic minor, and melodic minor scales should be practiced in all 12 keys.

Harmonized Major and Minor Scales

(practice in all 12 keys)

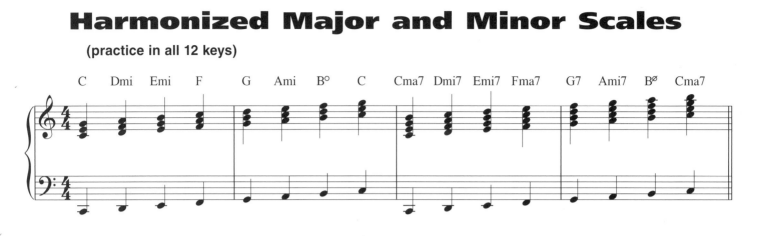

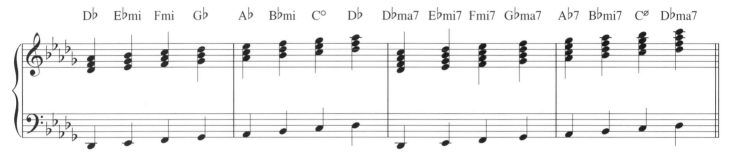

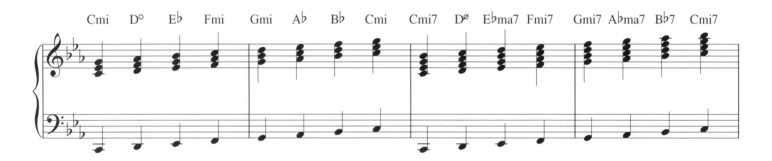

Modal Interchange

Modal interchange (also called "borrowed chords") refers to the practice of using chords from a mode (scale) other than the prevailing mode of a piece. In its most common form it means borrowing chords from the key parallel to the one you're in at any given point. For example, if a song is in the key of C major, modal interchange chords would be ones taken from the key of C minor. As a reminder, parallel keys are those that share the same tonic note (C major and C minor), as opposed to relative keys, which share the same key signature (C major and A minor).

The following figure shows a C major scale and a C natural minor scale, harmonized with triads. All the chords are interchangeable. (Exchanging the tonic chord, while theoretically possible, doesn't often happen, because it dilutes the sense of tonality too much.)

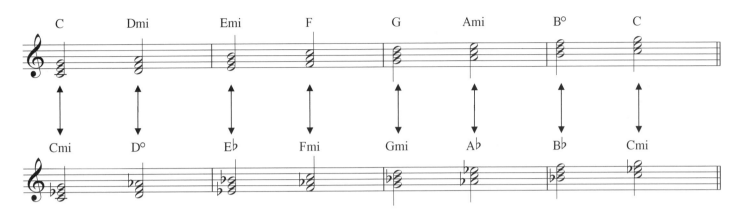

Modal interchange chords occur regularly in popular music. The following examples show several instances of modal interchange in otherwise diatonic progressions.

In the key of C major, the diatonic subdominant chord is F. This chord can be substituted for Fmi, which is the diatonic subdominant chord in the key of C minor. Note that the basic tonic–subdominant–tonic feel is retained, but with a different, more dissonant color.

In the next example, the diatonic IIImi chord in the key of C (Emi) is replaced by the ♭III chord (E♭) borrowed from C minor.

The next progression moves down in steps from the tonic chord. The first two bars show the diatonic version (I–VIIdim–VImi); in bars 3 and 4, the chords B♭ (♭VII) and A♭ (♭VI) are borrowed from the parallel minor key.

In the following example, the major keys' diatonic dominant chord is replaced with the one from the parallel minor key. This may seem counterintuitive because the leading tone gets substituted away, but it results in an interesting progression that is not uncommon.

In the last example, the key center is C minor. In bar 3, the subdominant chord of the parallel major key, F, is used instead of the diatonic Fmi chord.

While borrowing chords works in both directions, it is somewhat more common for songs in a major key to borrow chords from the parallel minor key than the other way around. In part, this is because in minor keys, a lot of the chords that occur in the parallel major key can also be derived from the harmonic or melodic minor scales; this eliminates the need for modal interchange. Because of the three different minor scales, minor keys have a much larger pool of diatonic chords to draw from. Major keys have only seven diatonic chords; therefore, there is greater necessity of additional harmonic material.

Secondary Dominants

Secondary dominant chords are another way to chromatically enhance diatonic progressions. They do this by exploiting the extraordinary strength of a chord resolving to another chord whose root is a perfect fourth higher. Earlier in this chapter, we got to know this harmonic movement as a dominant to tonic (V–I) progression. It is also possible to precede diatonic chords other than the tonic with their respective dominant chords. In other words, any chord in a key can be embellished by a major triad or dominant seventh chord whose root lies a perfect fifth above its own. For example, the IImi chord in the key of C, Dmi, can be preceded by its dominant, in this case A or A7. In terms of harmonic function, this A chord is called V/IImi, or V7/IImi (pronounced "five of two minor" or "five seven of two minor"). Similarly, the secondary dominant chord of the V chord in the key would be V/V or V7/V.

- In major keys, the dominant belonging with the tonic chord is already present. It can be considered the "primary dominant."

- The chord built on the seventh scale degree is not considered in the context of secondary dominants. This is because its quality is diminished, and diminished chords are too unstable to act, even temporarily, as a tonic in a dominant/tonic relationship.

- A tonic triad preceding the subdominant chord, although resolving up a perfect fourth and therefore forming a V/I relationship, is not considered a secondary dominant because, obviously, it is already present as a diatonic chord. However, a dominant seventh chord built on the tonic note (I7) is a chromatic chord; as such, it has to be analyzed as a secondary dominant seventh chord.

- That leaves the chords built on the second, third, fifth, and sixth scale degrees, all of which can be preceded by secondary dominant chords.

The following figures demonstrate secondary dominant triads and secondary dominant seventh chords in the key of C.

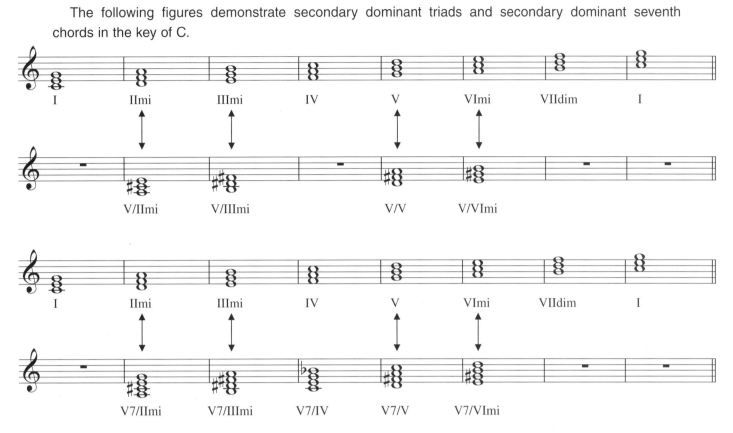

A dominant/tonic relationship always suggests a key center, especially when the dominant is a seventh chord. A secondary dominant chord, therefore, has the effect of temporarily hinting at a new key, without an actual modulation taking place. The sense of tonality prevails, but it is diluted enough to create harmonic ambiguity. This makes music less predictable. It also creates more tension (dissonance) by introducing chromatic notes into the progression, hence making the eventual resolution that much more satisfying.

There is one other important distinction regarding secondary dominants, and that is between functioning and non-functioning secondary dominants.

Functioning Secondary Dominant Chords

A secondary dominant chord is considered functioning if it is followed by its intended chord of resolution – in other words, if it resolves up a perfect fourth. In the key of C, for instance, an A7 chord progressing to Dmi is a functioning secondary dominant seventh chord.

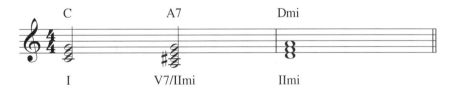

Non-functioning Secondary Dominant Chords

If a secondary dominant chord is not followed by the expected chord of resolution, it is considered non-functioning. The harmonic analysis remains the same; for example, an A7 chord in the key of C is considered V7/IImi, whether or not it progresses to IImi. The non-functioning variety of secondary dominants is less common than the functioning one, but it still happens quite frequently. The following example shows a non-functioning secondary dominant chord in the key of C; instead of resolving up a fourth to Ami (the VImi chord in the key of C), it is followed by an F major triad (the IV chord in the key of C):

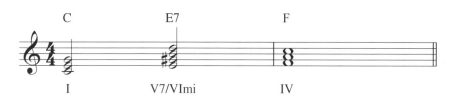

Secondary dominant chords are widely used in all styles of popular music. The examples below demonstrate their use in a number of harmonic progressions (an arrow denotes a functioning secondary dominant):

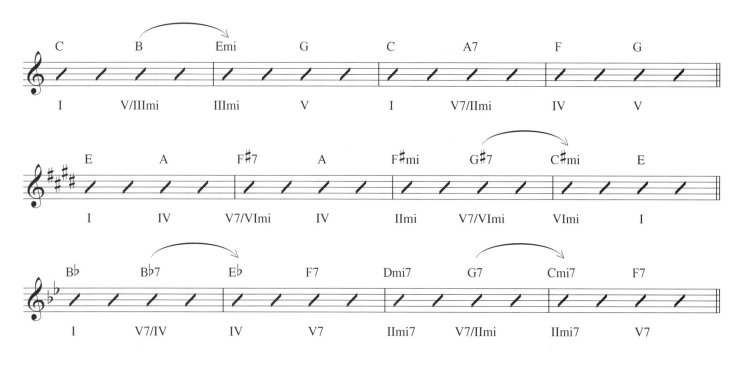

Modulation

The previous two categories, modal interchange chords and secondary dominant chords, expand on the strictly diatonic framework by introducing a measure of chromaticism without leaving the key center. By contrast, modulation is a technique by which the key of a piece of music is changed. While secondary dominants only hint at a different key, modulation firmly establishes a new key center, at least in theory. In practice, there is a measure of ambiguity and subjectivity involved. Certain progressions might be perceived as modulating to a new key by some listeners, but not by others. The length of the passage in the new key is probably the most important factor: After a certain amount of time spent in a different key, the ear is bound to lose its connection to the original key.

There are various types of modulation, the most important ones being pivot-chord modulation and direct modulation.

Pivot-Chord Modulation

In this case, the modulation takes place by means of a transitional chord that both keys have in common – one that can be analyzed as belonging to both the original key and the new key. This makes for a smooth transition. The pivot-chord can be diatonic in both keys (this is also called common-chord modulation), or it can be a modal interchange chord or a secondary dominant chord in one or both keys.

The examples below show several instances of pivot-chord modulation. The pivot chord itself is marked with an arrow:

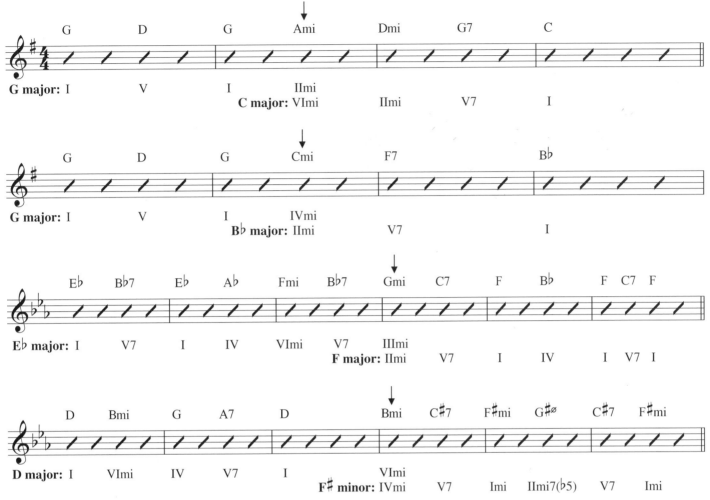

Direct Modulation

A direct modulation occurs abruptly, with no apparent common or pivot chord. It is simply a change to a new key center, with no hint in the preceding harmony that a change is about to occur. This is more dramatic than pivot-chord modulation, and can be striking.

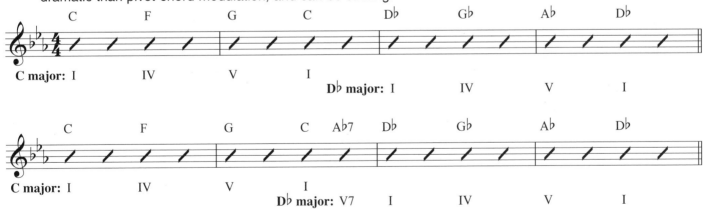

The most familiar occurrence of modulation in popular music is probably the big modulation chorus toward the end of a pop or R&B ballad. This is often referred to as "key change" in popular terminology. It is an arranging cliché that can work well when exercised with taste, but one should refrain from over-using it.

Chord Progressions

7

Voice Leading

When it comes to playing chord progressions on the keyboard, we first have to look at the concept of voice leading. Voice leading refers to the rules governing the movement from one harmony to the next.

As keyboard players, we are often tempted to look at a chord as a monolithic structure. We just drop our hands on the piano and play, say, a C major triad. But chords are made up of individual notes called voices; in order to understand voice leading, we have to consider them in those terms. Think of the triad as being sung by three singers (three voices!), each covering one note of the chord. The goal of good voice leading is for each individual note of a chord to move smoothly to a note of the next chord.

Let's say we have a chord progression of a C major triad moving to an F major triad. In the following example, both chords are voiced in root position:

This way of voicing the progression is not ideal, for two reasons: 1) it does not sound very smooth; 2) it is relatively awkward to play. (If you had to perform these two voicings in rapid succession, there'd be a lot of jumping around on the keyboard.)

So, what's a better way to play this? In the following example, the F chord is voiced as a second-inversion triad instead of a root-position triad:

This sounds much better, and it is easier to play. To determine the best inversions as you move from harmony to harmony, observe the following two rules:

- Common tones (notes that are present in both chords) should stay in the same octave and in the same voice.

- The other notes should move as short a distance as possible.

Let's apply these two rules to the example above. A C major triad and an F major triad share one common tone, C. In the first voicing, the root-position C major chord, that note C is middle C, and it is in the third voice of the chord. (Voices are counted from the top down.) That means that in the F voicing, it should be middle C, as well, and it should also be in the third voice. Then, the notes E and G should move as little as possible to F and A, respectively. The second example above fulfills all these requirements.

If there are no common tones between two successive chords, one often has two options that work equally well. In the next example, an F major triad is followed by a G major triad. These two chords don't share any common tones, so you can move up or down to the G chord:

In classical music, these rules are adhered to rather strictly. There are also more of them. In popular music, you can usually get by with the two basic rules I mentioned; there are also situations where other considerations overrule proper voice leading. Additionally, the more complex the harmonic structures get, the more complicated the voice-leading rules, and the more loosely they are applied. Just remember that when you're voicing simple three- or four-note chords, 90 percent of the time you'll want to consider proper voice leading.

Exceptions

Here are some examples of situations where you might want to ignore strict voice leading in favor of other considerations:

If you're harmonizing a melody, the melody note at any given time determines the voicing of the supporting chord. In the following example, a melody is harmonized with the same C to F progression from earlier. In this case, it makes sense to use root position on both chords because the melody note is the fifth of the chord:

Melodic movement interwoven with chordal playing is another recurrent technique; often, one will use the same voicing for the next chord, regardless of voice leading, in order to get the same melodic movement. In the following example, the top voice of the C major triad moves to a suspension and back to create interest; that same movement is applied to the following F and B♭ chords:

TRACK 1

In rock music, there is a lot of parallel harmonic movement, especially when there are power chords involved. This applies to guitar playing a lot more than keyboard playing (partly because of the way a guitar is laid out – it lends itself to moving chords around in a parallel fashion), but sometimes it is idiomatically correct to take the same approach on the keyboard.

TRACK 2

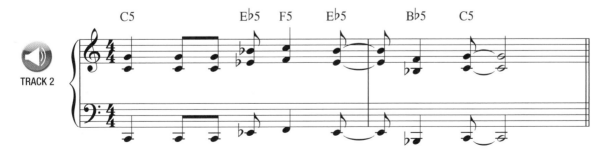

Root Movement

We can look at chord progressions from the perspective of root movement. Root movement refers to the interval between the root of a given chord and the root of the chord that follows.

Circle of Fifths

The Circle (or Cycle) of Fifths proceeds through all major and minor keys at intervals of a perfect fifth. It is usually presented in the context of key signatures, but it is also an established way to progress from chord to chord in songs. Sometimes it is referred to as the Circle of Fourths, the difference being the direction of the interval (a fifth up is equivalent to a fourth down, and vice versa). For the purpose of chord progressions, it doesn't matter whether you think of the movement as a fourth or a fifth. The progression from a C chord to a G chord can be thought of as moving up a fifth or moving down a fourth.

The following figure shows the Circle of Fifths with all major keys signatures:

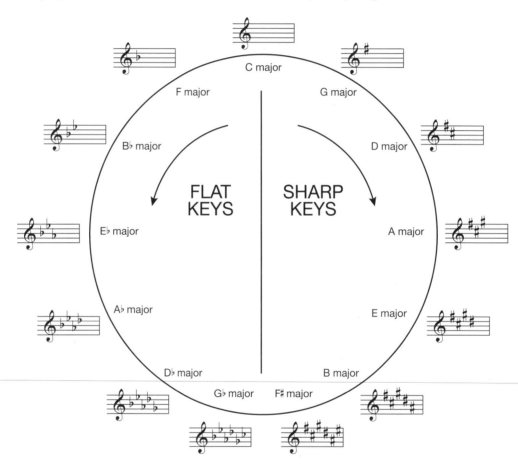

The closer the proximity of two chords on the Circle of Fifths, the more likely they are to occur next to each other in a chord progression. A C chord moving to an F chord (just one step removed on the circle) is much more likely than a C chord moving to an A♭ chord (four steps removed).

The next figure shows the Circle of Fifths again, this time with the relative minor keys next to the major keys:

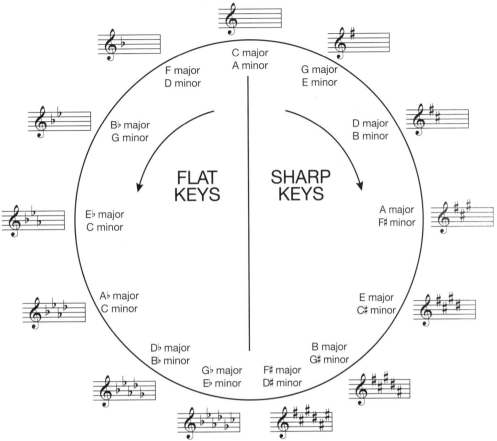

Moving from a C major chord to a D minor chord is common; again, you can see that those two chords are in close proximity on the Circle of Fifths. The most familiar progression in all of Western music is the movement from a tonic chord to a dominant chord – or the other way around, dominant to tonic.

Here is the same progression (tonic–dominant–tonic), but in a minor key:

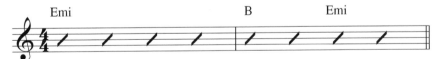

The movement from a tonic chord to a subdominant chord (or the other way around) is also ubiquitous.

Cycle progressions in which multiple chords move in intervals of a fourth up are very common. In the following example, the progression moves from D7 up a fourth to G7, then up a fourth to C7, and then up a fourth to Fma7:

Stepwise Movement

Stepwise movement occurs when the root of one chord moves to the root of the next chord by whole step or half step. Such movement can be diatonic or chromatic.

Diatonic movement occurs when a diatonic chord moves to the next one up or down the diatonic scale. In the key of C major, for example, the tonic chord C can move up to Dmi, which can move up to Emi, which can move up to F, and so on. Similarly, the chords can move down along the diatonic scale, as in F to Emi to Dmi to C.

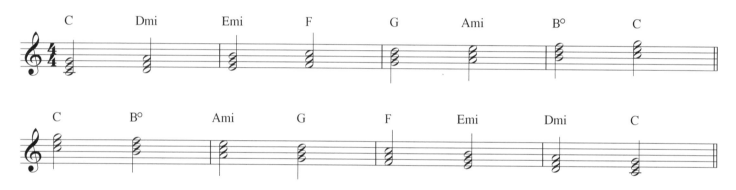

Chromatic stepwise movement occurs when at least one of the chord roots is non-diatonic. Oftentimes, two diatonic chords that are a whole step apart are connected by the chord whose root lies between them. For instance, in the key of C major, the diatonic IIImi and IImi chords can be connected chromatically.

Mediants – Movement in Thirds

The word mediant can refer to the third note of a scale, or the chord built on the third degree of a scale, or a root movement. Movement in thirds is quite frequent within the diatonic framework. For example, in the key of C major, the tonic chord C can move to Emi or Ami can move to F.

Tritone Movement

A tritone is the interval of a diminished fifth (or its enharmonic equivalent, an augmented fourth). Tritone root movement is not very smooth, and therefore considerably more rare than the options mentioned earlier. The most common occurrences are a I chord moving to a ♯IVmi7(♭5) chord and a progression known as tritone substitution, whereby a dominant seventh chord is followed by another dominant seventh chord a tritone away. (This is a staple in jazz progressions).

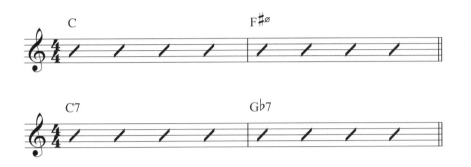

Pedal Point

The pedal point should be mentioned here. The pedal point (or "organ point," or "pedal" for short) originated in classical music. It is the practice of sustaining a bass note while the chords change on top of it. This was used extensively in organ literature, hence "organ point" or "pedal point;" organs have pedals that are played with the feet. Today this technique is used in every style of music.

Pedal Tone

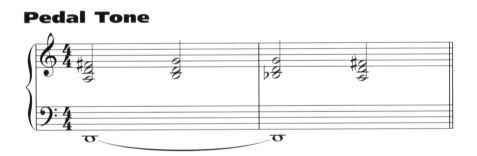

A variation of the regular pedal is the inverted pedal, whereby the pedal occurs in the top voice.

Inverted Pedal

By extension, the concept of pedals can be applied to motifs rather than just single notes. An example of this would be a constant bass ostinato (a short repeated figure) with chords changing on top of it.

Bass Ostinato Functioning as a Pedal

TRACK 3

Again, this can be inverted so that the constant figure is in a higher voice, and the bass notes change underneath. The electric guitar part in our example illustrates this: It plays a repeated figure using the notes A, E, B, and C♯, while the chords progress underneath.

Melodic Motif Functioning as Inverted Pedal

TRACK 4

Simply put, a pedal involves the juxtaposition of two musical elements, one of which is constant and one of which changes. This is a very common device in popular music.

Here are several examples of pedal point:

TRACK 5

TRACK 6

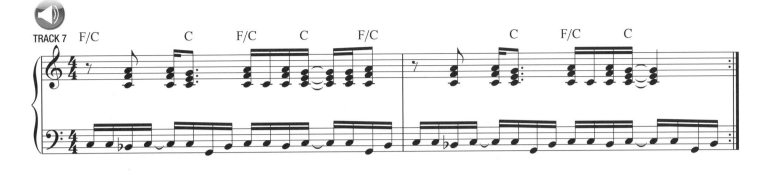

TRACK 7

TRACK 8

TRACK 9

TRACK 10

The following etude features common chord progressions with correct voice leading. Practice it in all 12 keys.

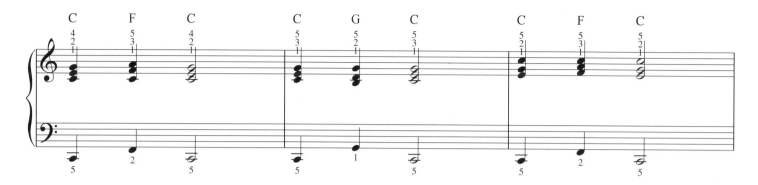

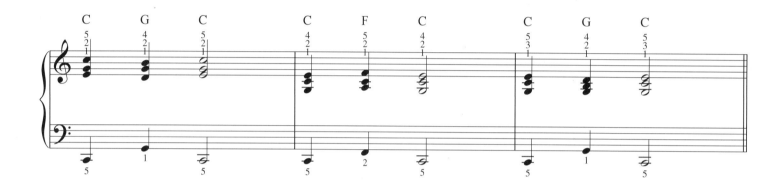

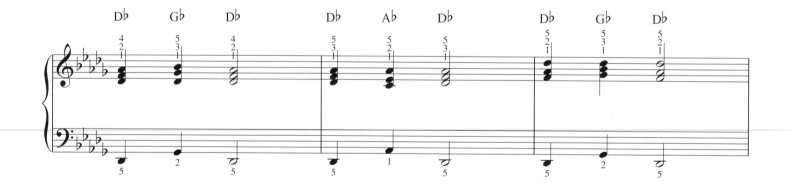

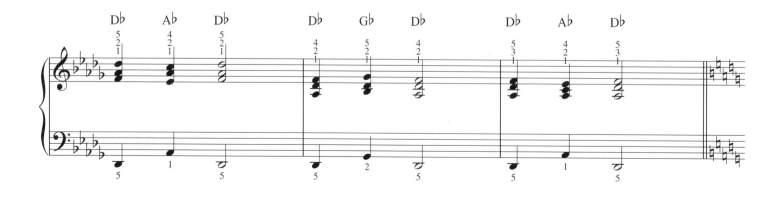

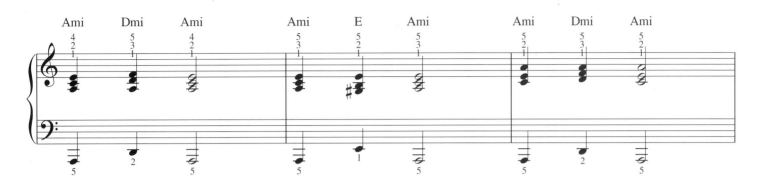

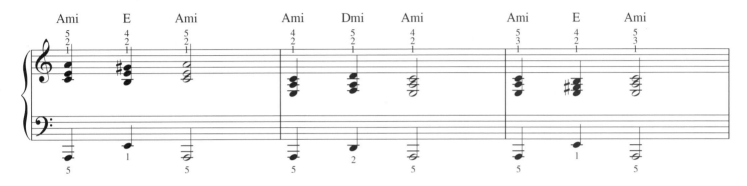

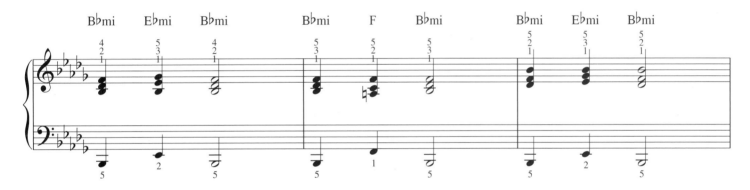

Part Three
Rhythm

Rhythm is one of the three main elements of music, in addition to melody and harmony. Humans have a primal connection to rhythm. Our bodies have various rhythms. We breathe in and out, in and out, in and out. We walk in a rhythm (left-right-left-right). While we're still in the womb, our mother's heartbeat quite literally signifies the "rhythm of life." Day and night, the tides, the seasons – we are surrounded by nature's rhythms everywhere.

Historically, drumming was most likely the first musical expression, other than singing. The first musical instruments were percussion instruments. Most people instinctively react to rhythmic music by tapping their feet, snapping their fingers, nodding their heads, or dancing.

Most of our music has a meter, which means that there is an underlying regular pulse, although some music is played with "free time" (also called *rubato*).

The following concepts are pertinent when discussing rhythm:

- meter

- subdivision

- syncopation

We will explore these elements one by one in the following chapters. After that, we'll look at the concept of harmonic rhythm (the rhythmic aspect of chord progressions) and rhythmic notation in popular music.

Meter

Most of our music is based upon a meter. In music, meter refers to a rhythmic pulse underlying the music, and involving a certain number of beats to a bar, and certain patterns of strong (accented) and weak beats within a bar.

In a 4/4 time signature, for example, each bar contains four quarter-note beats, with implied accents on the first and (to a slightly lesser extent) third beat of the bar.

When we listen to music, we instinctively pick up on this pulse, and then relate every note we hear to that pulse. In Western music, a 4/4 time signature is by far the most common. Others that occur frequently are 3/4 and 6/8. In 3/4, the accent is usually on the first beat of every bar. In 6/8 time, it is on the first and fourth eighth notes of each bar.

The symbol in the following example is sometimes used to signify 4/4 time:

The same symbol, but with a vertical line through it, means 2/2 time. This is also called "cut time" and is used for fast tempos.

Odd Meter

Odd-meter time signatures are rare in popular music. They are used somewhat more frequently in jazz and contemporary classical music. The most frequently used ones are 5/4 and 7/4. The fact that a whole bar cannot easily be divided by two makes them harder for us to relate to. Film music uses a lot of odd time signatures; their unstable and disconcerting sound often works well when underscoring a movie scene.

Chapter 8

Mixing Different Time Signatures

The mixing of different time signatures in the same piece is also relatively rare in pop music. Again, jazz and classical music are more complex in this regard (although, even in those styles, regular meters are far more frequent).

In pop songs, it's not unusual to insert an extra beat or two at the end of a section, thereby delaying the expected beginning of the next section. This can be very effective.

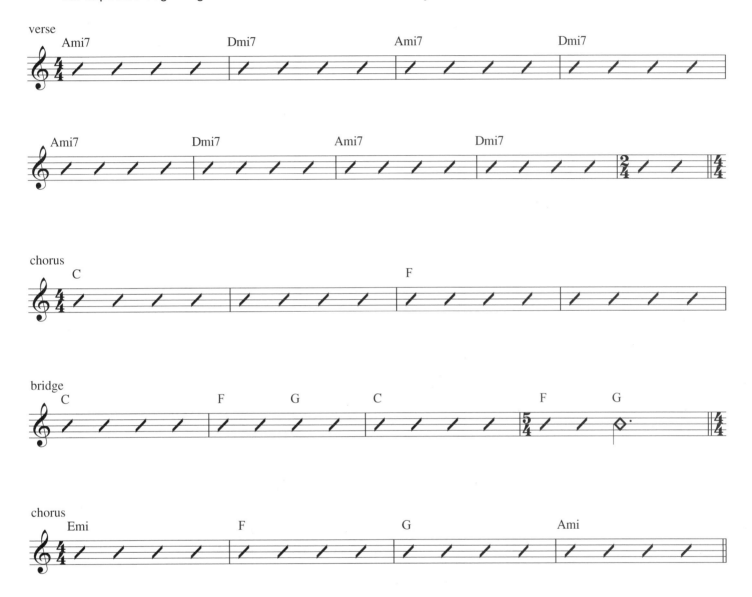

Subdivision

The regularity and predictability of a meter lends stability to the music. It anchors the temporal dimension of music, just like a diatonic key anchors it in terms of tonality. However, at some point the predictability of the regular meter needs to be broken, lest the music become boring. Here is a melody composed entirely of quarter notes, the basic rhythmic unit of the 4/4 time signature:

While this melody is not "wrong," it certainly is boring. Rhythmic variety is needed. One option is to introduce rests:

Adding rests made the melody a lot more musical, but in the long run, even the juxtaposition of quarter notes and quarter rests does not provide enough variety. This is where subdivision comes in.

Subdivision is the first step in rhythmic development, after establishing a meter. Each basic metric unit (in this case, quarter notes) can be divided in half to form two eighth notes, which can be further divided into 16th notes, and so on. Quarter notes can also be added up to form half notes and whole notes.

One can also divide a rhythmic value into three equal parts, thereby creating triplets. For example, one quarter note can be divided into two eighth notes or three eighth-note triplets.

Adding a dot to a note makes it longer by half of its original value. For example, a half note equals two quarter notes, whereas a dotted half note equals three quarter notes.

Chapter 9

Below, the previous melody has been rewritten using a variety of subdivisions:

After a while, even the variations shown here are not sufficient to keep the listener's interest. That is where the most important tool in the creation of rhythmic interest comes in: syncopation.

Syncopation

On a rhythmic level, the most powerful way to create tension – and its subsequent release – is syncopation. Syncopation is the obfuscation of the regular meter by emphasizing beats or subdivisions that are not normally accented. This has a disorienting effect on the listener and therefore demands attention. The subsequent return to the accenting of strong beats restores order in the rhythmic universe; the arc of consonance/dissonance/consonance is complete.

Syncopation can be achieved in three basic ways:

- By not playing a note where you expect one to be played; in other words, placing rests on a strong beat, or tying a note on a strong beat to the previous note.

- By playing a note on an offbeat, while at the same time leaving out the expected strong beat before or after.

- By accenting notes you would not expect to be accented.

The following examples illustrate these various forms of syncopation.

In the first example, no note is played on beat 3. This implicitly puts accents on the notes before and after, on beats 2 and 4, thereby disrupting the expected pattern of accents on beats 1 and 3:

In the next example, the same effect is achieved by placing a half note on beat 2, which extends over beat 3, once again leaving beat 3 unaccented:

In the following example, the note on beat 4 of the first bar is tied over to the note on beat 1 of the second bar. Beat 4 of the first bar and beat 2 of the second bar are given more weight because of the missing beat in between them:

In the next example, the note on 2+ is tied to the note on beat 3. Musicians call this "pushing the 3," meaning the expected note on beat 3 is instead anticipated and played on the second eighth note of beat 2:

In the example below, the last 16th note of beat 2 is tied to the note on beat 3. Again, beat 3 is pushed, this time by a 16th note, which creates even stronger syncopation than the pushed eighth note in the previous example:

In the following example, several accented offbeats in a row create strong syncopation. Instead of the expected notes on the strong beats 2, 3, and 4, there are notes on 1+, 2+, 3+, and 4+:

The more syncopated notes we hear in a row, the stronger the rhythmic disorientation. Eventually, the tension needs to be relieved by a note on a regular strong beat, otherwise the listener will lose his connection to the original meter, and turn the beat around in his head. Knowing how far one can take syncopation in any given context is part of a musician's compositional or improvisational skill set.

Although there are myriad possible rhythms, there are some that happen quite frequently. We will examine them in the following examples.

Pushing by an Eighth Note

We can create rhythmic momentum if we anticipate a strong beat by an eighth note, a technique used over and over in pop music. For example, instead of playing on beat 3, one can play on 2+ instead. Beat 3 will either have a rest, or the note on 2+ will sustain over beat 3.

Anticipation by an eighth note works with all downbeats (1, 2, 3, and 4 in a bar of 4/4).

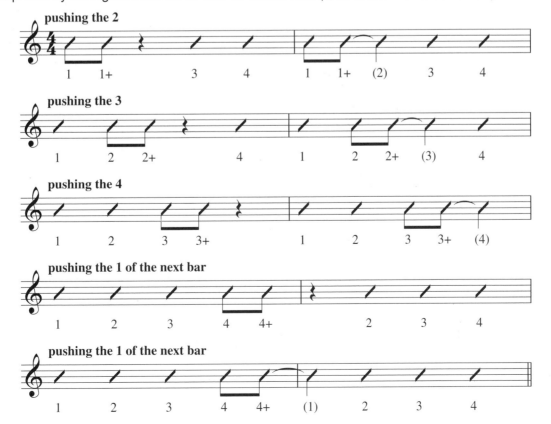

Pushing by a 16th Note

Downbeats can be anticipated by a 16th note. This works in a similar fashion to pushing by an eighth note, and it is also used frequently.

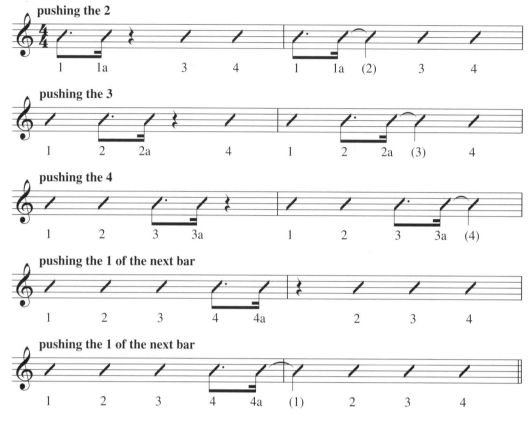

Sometimes a two-bar or four-bar phrase will feature the same syncopation in every bar, as illustrated in the example below. The frequent "pushes" create a lot of momentum and propel the music forward:

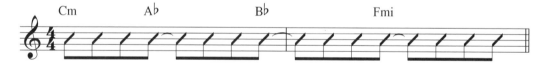

Implied Syncopation

In the example below, a continuous eighth-note rhythm is punctuated by accents. Although not technically syncopation, because all the strong beats are present, the effect is similar.

The technique of creating syncopation by placing accents on various beats of a continuous eighth-note or 16th-note pattern is used a lot in popular music. A continuous eighth-note rhythm of power chords, played on an electric guitar and punctuated by accents that create the appearance of syncopation, is a common example.

Another important way of creating quasi-syncopated rhythms is demonstrated below. The first bar features a melodic line of continuous eighth notes, four on the note B, and then four on the note G. In the second bar, the melody note changes on 2+ instead of 3. This creates the illusion of syncopation, in spite of the fact that, strictly speaking, none is present:

The same effect can be achieved with chord progressions. In the following example, the chord changes on the 3+, again creating the illusion of syncopation, without there actually being any:

Rhythmic Notation

11

Rhythm has been an integral part of music notation for centuries. Traditionally, almost every note had a pitch and a rhythmic value. However, in contemporary notation, especially on chord charts, you'll find a lot of notes that have only a rhythmic value and no specific pitch. These are called rhythm slashes; they are used to tell the musicians what rhythm to play without telling them specifically which note (or notes) to play. Oftentimes, there is a basic rhythmic figure or a specific syncopation that the players should be aware of, but there is no need to write out which pitches to play. For that, the musicians will consult the chord symbols, and then improvise a part that is idiomatically correct relative to their instrument and the style of the song. Interpreting slash notation on chord charts is an important skill any pop musician should possess.

The following shows one bar of typical rhythm slash notation, with chord symbols written above the staff:

Here's how various musicians might execute that bar on their respective instruments:

It is important to note that most parts in the example above contain more notes than the slash notation suggests, although the bass part and the left hand of the piano part follow the slash notation literally. This illustrates that slash notation does not necessarily mean "Play only this exact rhythm and nothing else." Rather, it often means "Interpret this rhythm in a musically appropriate fashion." Sometimes that interpretation will include only the given slash rhythm, and sometimes it will include other notes filling in the space around it. The players' experience and idiomatic ability dictate when to do what.

Chapter 11

In part, the amount of latitude in interpreting slash notation is instrument-specific. For instance, drummers almost always play filler notes, whereas bass players (or the keyboard player's left hand) usually play only the notated slash rhythm. Bear in mind, though, that these are generalizations. In the end, it comes down to the individual situation, song, and player.

In rhythm notation, there is an important distinction between rhythms that pertain to the entire band, and rhythms that pertain to one (or a group of) instrument(s) only. Chord charts usually contain only rhythms that concern the whole band. In master rhythm charts or hybrid charts, you can be more specific. If you write individual parts for all instruments, you can tell each player exactly what to play.

Rhythm can be more important than pitch in terms of accurate representation of a song. In rhythm guitar parts or keyboard parts, for example, playing the exact rhythm with a different voicing than the original part usually sounds more authentic than playing the exact voicing, but with a different rhythm.

There are two kinds of rhythm slashes: 1) slashes without stems; 2) slashes with stems.

Rhythm Slashes without Stems

Rhythm slashes without stems are used in a specific capacity. They don't denote any particular rhythms. Rather, they are placeholders filling up bars, telling the musicians to "Play something in the style of the song, using the chord symbols provided." (In musicians' vernacular, this is called "playing time.") In other words, they tell you to play, but not what to play. (Depending on the instrument, the player could also decide not to play in spite of the rhythm slashes. Sometimes the best contribution you can make is silence.) Again, all this relies heavily on the experience, musicality, and creativity of the musicians.

If the basic metric unit (represented by the bottom number in the time signature) is quarter note (by far the most common), half note, or whole note, one uses quarter notes for the rhythm slashes. However, if the metric unit is eighth note (as in 6/8), or even 16th note, then those smaller note values are used for rhythm slashes. In those cases, one uses slash notation with stems.

Rhythm Slashes with Stems

Rhythm slashes with stems are used to denote specific rhythms, while leaving the choice of notes to the performer's discretion. How a musician will interpret this notation depends on several variables, most notably the instrument and the style of the music. Harmony instruments such as guitars or keyboards usually play some form of chordal accompaniment using the specified rhythm. Bassists incorporate the rhythm into the bass line. Drummers often play a lot of filler notes surrounding the specified rhythm, while putting special emphasis on the notated rhythm.

It is a common scenario for a chord chart to feature mostly stemless rhythm slashes (telling the musicians to "play time") and the occasional bar of slashes with stems (telling the musicians to play a specific rhythm). The following example shows the juxtaposition of rhythm slashes with and without stems, as you might find in a chart:

Notice that half notes and whole notes get diamond-shaped note heads when turned into slashes.

It is possible to combine slashes with and without stems in the same measure, as in the next example:

Again, slash notation doesn't always have to be taken literally, as in "I'm not allowed to play a single note that is not notated in this slash rhythm." Experienced musicians know that in interpreting this kind of notation, it is perfectly acceptable to play filler notes surrounding the main rhythm.

Part Four
Melody

There are two basic ways we keyboard players interface with the concept of melody. First, by playing a given melody that's part of a composition, and that's often written out. Second, by improvising a melody, whether it's playing a solo, playing fills behind the main melody, or integrating melodic elements into comping patterns. The latter is the more difficult task, because in addition to technical chops, it requires the ability to "compose" coherent melodies on the fly according to certain parameters. Therefore, in this fourth part of the book we'll focus on improvising melodies in a pop music context.

We will mainly discuss improvising over chord changes, as that is what you will be doing most of the time when you improvise. There are a number of concepts, which, if mastered, will enable you to navigate almost any song or chord progression.

While improvisation over chord progressions may seem like a vast subject, almost all of it can be reduced to the mastery of the following practical and conceptual elements, at least in pop music.

Practical

- You must be able to play a (relatively small) number of scales in all keys.

- You must be able to play a (relatively small) number of chord shapes in all keys.

Conceptual

- You must understand the distinction between horizontal playing and vertical playing.

- You must understand key center improvisation (mostly horizontal), chord/scale improvisation (mostly vertical), and chord shape improvisation (vertical or horizontal).

We will discuss all these topics and use practical examples to illustrate these different ways of looking at improvising over chord progressions. The approach to use in any given situation depends on a variety of factors – including the chord progression itself, the style of the song, and personal preference. In some situations, using only one particular approach works well, but more often than not musicians use two or more over the course of a solo. While there are no hard-and-fast rules as to how to approach a particular chord progression, listening to and analyzing keyboard solos yields certain guidelines. There are things that everybody does, simply because they work. For example, using a blues scale to solo over a blues progression just works. That is not to say that we as musicians should always do what's common. Playing the same old thing all the time can sound uninspired and repetitive. You want to strike a balance between the tried and true and the adventurous. Again, where exactly that balance is depends on the song, the style, and your personal taste as an artist. When you're soloing over a country song, you have to color inside the lines a lot more than when you're playing a jazz standard. Part of the art of improvisation is knowing when to do what – or what to do when.

12 Scales and Chord Shapes

There are 12 notes in our musical system. While it is your prerogative to use all of them when composing or improvising a melody, it is more practical to narrow your melodic source material to a selection from those 12 notes, especially in popular music. The most pervasive selections in Western music are the major and minor scales and triads based on the diatonic system, covered in Part One of this book.

As mentioned in the Introduction, the elements we'll use for improvisation are several scales, and several chord shapes.

Scales

Music students are often overloaded with a multitude of different scales, especially in the study of jazz. In my opinion, 99 percent of any pop chord progression you will ever solo over can be covered with four scales. In the case of modes derived from a scale, I count only one scale. For example, the Dorian mode, despite being fairly widespread, is just a major scale played from the second scale degree. Therefore, I don't consider it a separate scale you have to learn.

Here are the four scales (and their derivatives) that you absolutely, positively have to know *in all 12 keys*:

- The major scale and its modes (Dorian, Phrygian, Lydian, Mixolydian, Aeolian [natural minor scale], and Locrian)

- The harmonic minor scale

- The melodic minor scale and three of its modes (Lydian flat seven, Locrian sharp two, and the altered scale)

- The minor pentatonic scale and the blues scale (The blues scale simply adds one chromatic step to a minor pentatonic scale.)

Practicing these four scales in all 12 keys might still seem challenging, but it is a far cry from having to practice the dozens of different scales that are sometimes thrown at unsuspecting music students.

It bears repeating that even though there are different names for the modes of a scale, they all contain the same notes and therefore don't have to be practiced as separate scales. This is especially important in regards to the melodic minor scale, which is usually not thought of as having modes (like the major scale). However, some of the most important contemporary scales are derivatives of the melodic minor scale.

Chord Shapes

Chord shapes are the second fundamental source of melodic material for improvisation. As with scales, there are many of them; as with scales, you really only have to practice a manageable number of them. They are several triadic chord shapes containing three notes (major, minor, augmented, diminished, and suspended), and several seventh chord shapes containing four notes (major seventh, dominant seventh, minor seventh, minor seventh flat five, diminished seventh, and minor major seventh). We already know all these shapes from Part Two of this book.

The Major Scale

Using the seven notes of a major scale as source material is a very common way to construct melodies. The different notes of the scale have certain degrees of dissonance and tendencies of resolution, but all of them work well together.

Modes

In popular music, we regularly base melodies on modes rather than official major or minor tonality. The Dorian and Mixolydian modes in particular are ubiquitous, especially in rock and R&B music. In jazz music, a lot of different modes are used for compositional purposes.

Writing a piece "in D Dorian," for example, rather than the traditional D major or D minor keys, can open up interesting new avenues for composition. In the following example, both the melody and the chords are based on the D Dorian scale.

TRACK 11

Minor Scales

As we've seen, in minor keys things are more complex than in major keys, because there are several different minor scales, each of which fits different harmonic situations.

The Natural Minor Scale

In minor keys, it is most common to use the natural minor scale as source material. Regarding the hierarchy of notes within the scale, the observations made about the major scale also apply. The major seventh scale degree, or leading tone, is one important note the natural minor scale doesn't provide. Thus, the harmonic minor scale was invented specifically for the purpose of providing a leading tone for minor keys.

The Harmonic Minor Scale

The harmonic minor scale is not quite as universally applicable as the major or natural minor scales. Its main function is to provide the leading tone, which is most often over the dominant chord of the key. The interval between the minor sixth and the major seventh of the scale is an augmented second. It does not sound smooth melodically and needs to be treated with discretion.

The Melodic Minor Scale

Typically, the melodic minor scale is not a source for melody notes in pop songs, but in other styles it can be effective. Jazz melodies are often based on the melodic minor scale and its modes. The juxtaposition of a minor third and a major sixth and seventh in the same scale creates a beautifully distinct sound.

The Dorian Mode

The Dorian mode, while not an independent minor scale in traditional music theory, is very common in popular and jazz music. If all you're soloing over is a tonic minor triad or minor seventh chord, the Dorian mode is frequently the best choice. Sometimes you have to experiment to determine whether the natural minor scale or the Dorian mode sounds better in the context of the song. The presence of a IV or IV7 chord is a good indication that Dorian is appropriate. Many songs or sections of songs use the chord progression Imi–IV, or Imi7–IV7. Dorian is always a good choice in these cases.

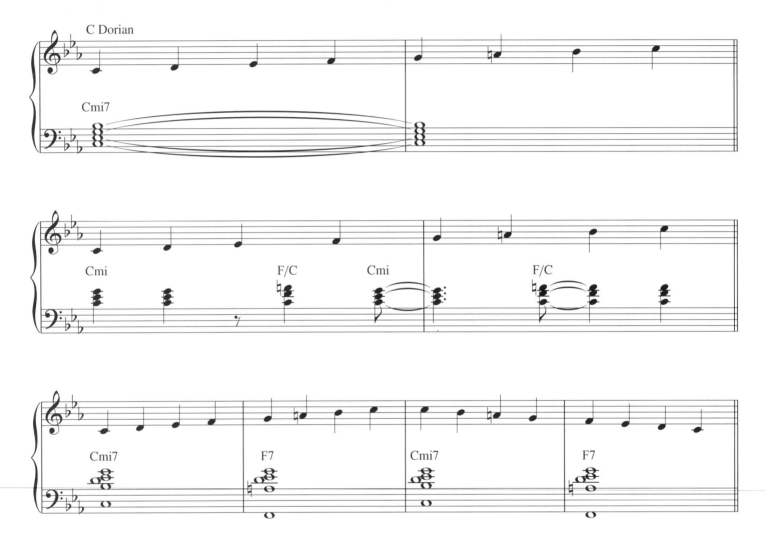

The two notes where the four minor scales differ are the sixth and the seventh. The melody often provides clues as to which scale to choose. The sixth, especially, is important in this context. A minor sixth in the melody suggests natural minor as the best scale choice for the tonic chord. A major sixth suggests Dorian. Ultimately, your ear has the final word.

The Blues Scale

The blues scale is one of the most important elements of contemporary improvisation. It is used in practically every style of popular music. Most of the time, the blues scale is used in a horizontal capacity – in other words, in the context of key-center playing. That means you usually play the blues scale built on the tonic of the key you are in rather than the blues scale built on the tonic of each individual chord. Note that there is another key-center-related blues scale on the submediant; we will examine that later.

The progression below contains three dominant seventh chords: A7, D7, and E7. These chords are the I, IV, and V chords in the key of A. The fact that all of them are dominant seventh chords immediately suggests a blues or blues-related song. Most of the time, you would play the tonic blues scale (in this case, the A blues scale) over all three chords, as opposed to playing an A and a D and an E blues scale.

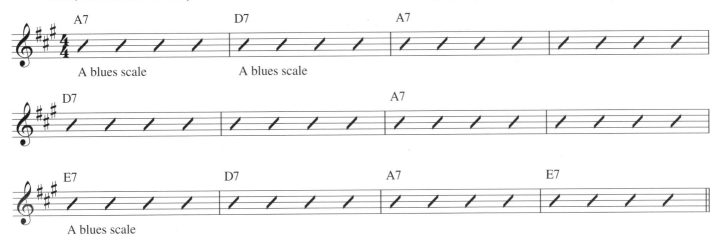

Knowing when to use the blues scale is a matter of experience and personal taste. There are certain situations where the blues scale is the obvious choice, and other times where you can choose to use it or not. The following harmonic situations lend themselves well to use of the tonic blues scale:

A) **Blues songs.** Obviously. Most commonly, these are 12-bar progressions, although there are blues tunes that have eight, 16, or 24 bars, among others. These songs make heavy use of dominant seventh chords built on the first, fourth, and fifth scale degrees. The example below is a jazzy blues progression. The chord progression is more complex, but it still contains strategically placed dominant seventh chords on I, IV, and V. The blues scale would be an excellent choice to improvise over the entire progression.

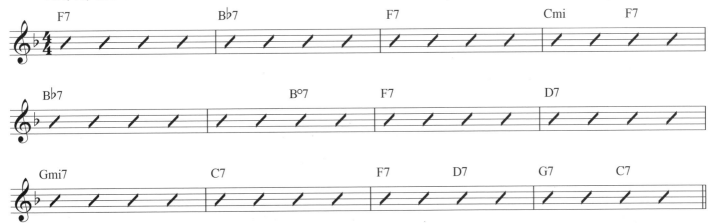

B) **Minor blues songs.** These are structurally similar to the above-mentioned blues songs, but they are built on minor tonality:

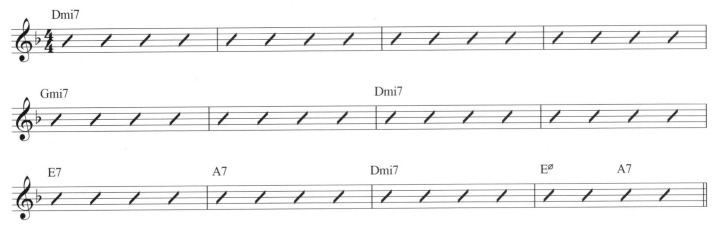

C) Songs or sections of songs that have only one chord, either a dominant seventh chord or a minor seventh chord. This almost always works with dominant seventh chords. With minor seventh chords, one has to be a little more discerning, but the blues scale is still an option that works in many cases.

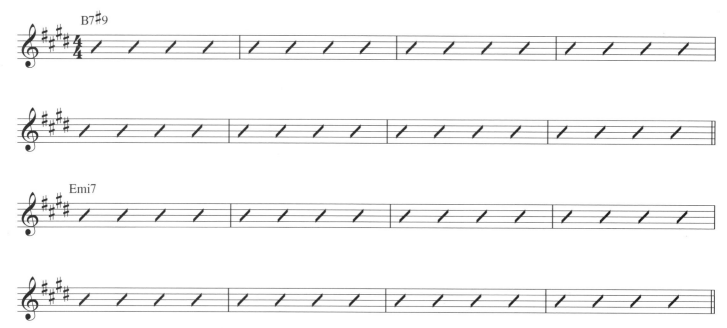

D) Songs or sections of songs that contain dominant seventh chords built on the first and/or fourth and/or fifth scale degree. For example, progressions routinely alternate between dominant chords on the first and fourth degrees of the tonic scale. The blues scale works well in this scenario.

E) Songs or sections of songs that contain the following chromatic (non-diatonic) dominant seventh chords: ♭II7, II7 (especially in minor keys), ♭III7, ♭VI7, VI7, and ♭VII7. This works best when these dominant chords are of relatively short duration, no more than a bar or two. The progression below revolves around the tonic C. It contains several chromatic dominant seventh chords, and the C blues scale is used to solo over all of them. Remember that this is a horizontal approach to soloing; not all notes make sense individually when played against the underlying chord, but the strength of the tonic blues scale and the sense of tonality that it creates make up for those dissonances.

TRACK 12

TRACK 13

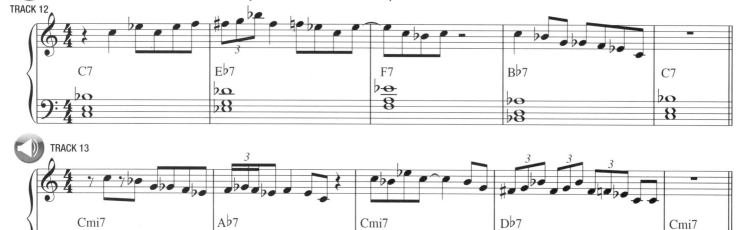

F) **Turnaround progressions.** Turnarounds usually happen at the end of a song or section of a song. They are harmonic progressions that start on a chord and then cycle through a few chords, leading back either to the first chord (this is the most common version) or to another chord (oftentimes a II or V chord). Each individual chord of the turnaround is usually one, two, or four beats long. Because of their short duration, it is often impractical to play a different scale on each chord. Key center works better, and the blues scale works particularly well. The example below shows a few typical turnarounds. In the first system, the progression starts out on a tonic dominant seventh chord and moves through a few other chords before returning to the C7 chord. In the second system, the starting and end points are tonic minor chords. In the third system, the starting point is a tonic sixth chord (C6); the turnaround moves through a few chords and arrives at the IImi7 (Dmi7) chord.

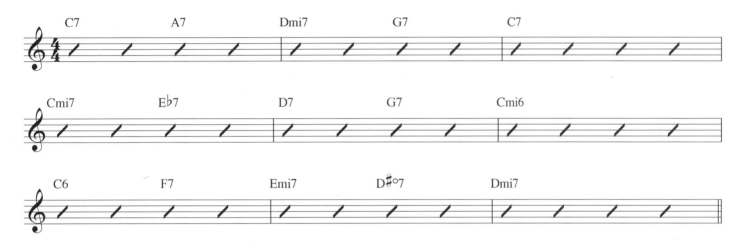

The Submediant Blues Scale

In addition to the blues scale built on the tonic, the one built on the submediant (the sixth degree of the scale) is quite important. Unlike the tonic blues scale, this one does not work for minor blues tunes or minor seventh chords. However, on tonic dominant seventh chords or blues-related progressions, it works well. Sometimes the submediant blues scale is even preferable to the tonic blues scale. It is less dissonant and is often used in situations where the tonic blues scale would sound too dissonant or too bluesy.

As an example, over a C7 chord or a blues in the key of C, you can play the A blues scale. (A is the sixth degree of a C major scale.)

This scale contains both a minor and a major third (relative to the tonic). That's one of its advantages. In this case, it contains both E♭ and E. Many blues phrases involve both the minor third and the major third.

TRACK 14

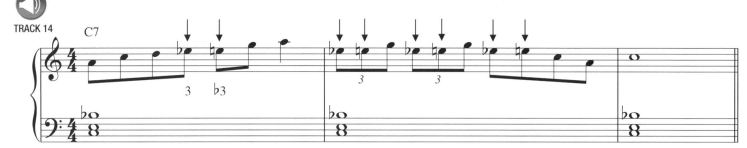

You have to be careful not to use the major third (of the key) when you're playing on the IV7 chord. One of the most pervasive harmonic movements in blues is I7–IV7. Oftentimes, players will melodically mark the difference between these two chords by playing the major third of the key on the I7 chord and the minor third of the key on the IV7 chord.

Both major and minor 3rd sound good over I7.   Avoid the major 3rd over IV7.

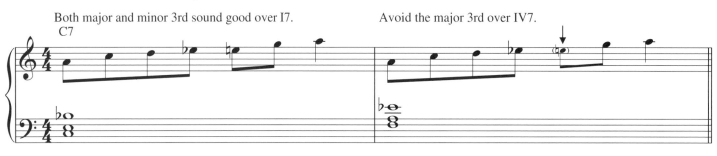

TRACK 15   Major and minor 3rds used to mark the difference between I7 and IV7.

When you build phrases with the submediant blues scale, it is best to anchor your melodies around the tonic of the key, rather than the tonic of the scale. In other words, when you play the A blues scale over a C7 chord, play the notes of the A blues scale, but treat the note C as if it were the root.

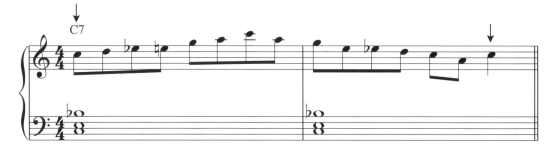

There are two ways to look at the individual notes of the submediant blues scale:

- In relation to the tonic chord or key

- In relation to the root of the submediant blues scale

Using the key of C and the A blues scale as an example, each note of the scale can be analyzed in relation to the tonic of the key (C) or the root of the scale (A). I usually think of the submediant blues scale (in this case the A blues scale), but with an emphasis on the second note (in this case the note C), which is the tonic of the key or the underlying chord structure. In the following example, the submediant blues scale is analyzed in relation to its root (bar 1) and to the root of the underlying tonality (bar 2).

Let's look at how the submediant blues scale can be applied to the various progressions discussed above.

A) **Blues songs.** The submediant blues scale is a good fit for blues progressions like the one below. You can use it to improvise over the entire progression, with one little caveat: Try to avoid using the fifth of the scale (the major third of the key you're in) on the IV7 chord. In the case of a blues in F, this means to avoid the note A on the B♭7 chord.

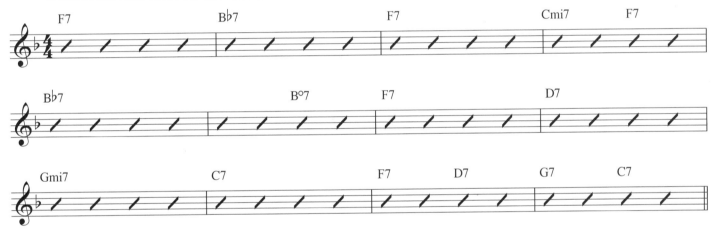

B) **Minor blues songs.** On minor blues tunes, the submediant blues scale does not work.

C) **Songs or sections of songs that contain only a dominant seventh chord.** The submediant blues scale almost always works with dominant seventh chords that function as a tonic chord. Unlike the tonic blues scale, however, this does not work with minor seventh chords.

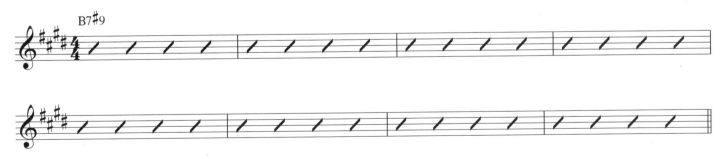

D) **Songs or sections of songs that contain dominant seventh chords built on the first and/or fourth and/or fifth scale degree.** The submediant blues scale works well in this scenario. The aforementioned exception applies here as well: Don't use the major third of the key over the IV7 chord.

E) **Songs or sections of songs that contain the following chromatic (non-diatonic) dominant seventh chords: II7, III7, and VI7.** As with the tonic blues scale, this works best when these dominant chords are of relatively short duration (no more than a bar or two). The example below revolves around the tonic C. It contains several chromatic dominant seventh chords, and the A blues scale is used to solo over all of them. This is a horizontal approach to soloing; not all notes make sense individually when played against the underlying chord, but the strength of the blues scale and the sense of tonality that it creates make up for those dissonances.

TRACK 16

TRACK 17

F) **Turnaround progressions.** Over turnaround progressions, the submediant blues scale works even better than the tonic blues scale. The example below shows eight bars' worth of turnarounds in the key of C. The A blues scale is used exclusively for soloing over them. The left hand plays a walking bass line in the first four bars. This example should be played with a swing feel.

TRACK 18

The Composite Blues Scale

So far, we have used the tonic and subdominant blues scales exclusively, in their pure forms. While it is not uncommon to use these scales for a few bars or even a chorus, if you do it for too long, the solo will get predictable und uninteresting. Most blues phrases draw from both aforementioned blues scales; sometimes you may also use notes not contained in either scale.

Combining the notes from both the tonic and subdominant blues scales creates the following composite blues scale:

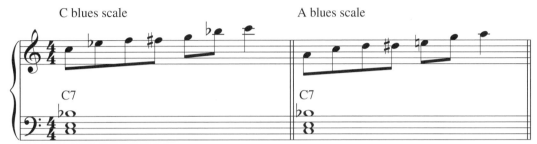

The composite blues scale combines notes from both the tonic and submediant blues scales:

The composite blues scale opens up a whole new range of melodic possibilities you don't get from either the tonic or submediant blues scales by themselves. Let's look at a few of them.

In the tonic blues scale, the lower neighbor tone of the tonic is flat seven. In the submediant blues scale, it is six. The composite blues scale provides both those notes.

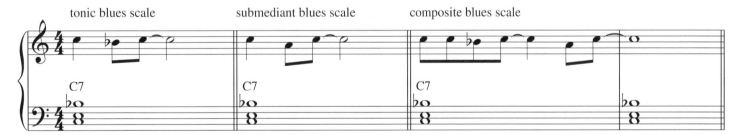

Embellishment of the major third using neighbor tones and enclosure is one of the most important melodic elements in blues playing. The tonic blues scale does not contain the major third at all; that's one of the reasons you don't want to use this scale exclusively for too long. The submediant blues scale contains both the major and minor third of the key, which is one of the reasons it is so useful. The composite blues scale contains the major third and both the upper and lower neighbor tones, thereby allowing for numerous ways to embellish the third.

Here are several typical blues phrases that contain embellishment of the major third:

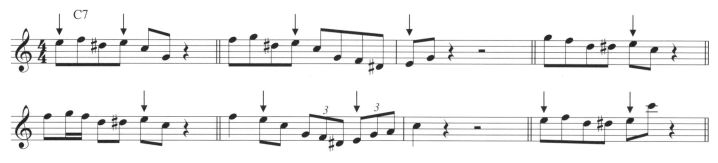

Another important melodic fragment derived from the composite blues scale is the chromatic movement from the third to the fifth.

Lastly, the composite blues scale contains the scale fragment 5-6-♭7-8, which provides a lot of melodic material.

The composite blues scale can be used in all situations that fit the regular tonic or submediant blues scales. When you play a regular blues scale up and down, it works melodically – to a certain extent – because of the leaps inherent in it. (Don't overdo this, however.) On the other hand, the composite blues scale should be looked at more as a pool of possible notes from which to choose, not as a scale in the traditional sense that can be played up and down.

The Pentatonic Scale

Pentatonic scales are ubiquitous in contemporary improvisation. They have been around at least since antiquity. The word pentatonic is Greek and means five (penta) notes (tonic). Pentatonic scales can be found all over the world. They occur in indigenous music, folk music, classical music, jazz, and pop. There are many variations, but we will focus on the most conventional ones: the major and minor pentatonic scales.

The figure below shows a C major pentatonic scale:

This scale can be viewed as an incomplete major scale. The fourth and seventh degrees are left out, thereby removing the two most dissonant notes from the scale.

The major pentatonic scale contains no half steps or tritone intervals. It contains the notes of the underlying tonic triad (C-E-G) and two relatively consonant notes that are often added on to major triads, the second (or ninth) and the sixth.

Here is a C minor pentatonic scale:

This scale can be viewed as an incomplete natural minor scale. The second and sixth degrees are left out, thereby removing the two most dissonant notes from the scale.

Analogously to the major pentatonic scale, the minor pentatonic scale contains no half steps or tritone intervals. It contains the notes of the underlying tonic triad (C-E♭-G) and two relatively consonant notes, the fourth and the minor seventh.

Similar to the relationship between a major scale and its relative minor scale, a major pentatonic scale contains the same notes as the minor pentatonic starting a minor third lower. For instance, the C major pentatonic scale contains the same notes as the A minor pentatonic scale.

Since the notes in relative major and minor pentatonic scales are identical, there is no need to practice them separately. I think in minor pentatonic because it is a lot more common than the major pentatonic. In other words, when practicing scales as part of your technique, it is enough to practice minor pentatonic scales. If I need to play, say, a C major pentatonic, I think of it as the second mode of the A minor pentatonic scale.

It is important to note that a pentatonic scale differs only slightly from a blues scale. If you omit the chromatic step between the fourth and fifth scale degree of a blues scale, you're left with a minor pentatonic scale.

This similarity between the blues scale and the minor pentatonic scale has implications that will be explained in the following chapters.

Because of the aforementioned close relationship between the blues scale and the pentatonic scale, almost everything that has been said about the use of the blues scale also applies to the pentatonic scale. The major pentatonic scale is similar to the submediant blues scale; like that blues scale, it can be used to solo over blues progressions, dominant chords with tonic function, and turnaround progressions.

The example below shows the similarity between a C major pentatonic scale and an A blues scale (the submediant blues scale) played over a C7 chord:

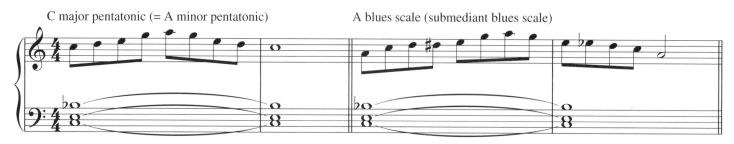

As stated earlier, I think in minor pentatonic, so even though I am aware that I am playing a C major pentatonic in the example above, in terms of the patterns and melodies I've practiced, I am thinking A minor pentatonic.

The example below shows the use of the E♭ major pentatonic scale (or C minor pentatonic scale) over a turnaround progression in the key of E♭:

TRACK 19

Because of the missing chromatic passing tone, the pentatonic scale sounds more generic than the blues scale. Therefore, it is often used where the blues scale would sound too dissonant or evoke too much of a bluesy feel. In pop songs, the major pentatonic scale is a frequent choice over tonic major triads or diatonic progressions anchored around the tonic triad. The example below shows the use of the E major pentatonic scale (or C♯ minor pentatonic) over a pop progression in the key of E major:

TRACK 20

The minor pentatonic scale can be used anywhere the blues scale can be used: on blues progressions, minor blues progressions, progressions containing dominant chords on the first, fourth, and fifth scale degrees, and turnarounds. Refer to earlier sections and simply substitute the minor pentatonic scale for the blues scale.

In addition, the minor pentatonic scale sounds good on tonic minor triads and diatonic minor key progressions. The following example shows the use of a G minor pentatonic scale over a mostly triadic progression in the key of G minor:

TRACK 21

The pentatonic scale has another big advantage worth mentioning. Unlike heptatonic scales (seven-note scales like the major or natural minor scales) or blues scales, the notes of the major or minor pentatonic scale can all be played with the sustain pedal down without creating too much dissonance. This comes in handy in pop music. A "wash of sound" is a standard stylistic device that can be compelling if not overused. The following example shows the use of a D minor pentatonic scale over a tonic D minor triad. Note the pedal markings:

TRACK 22

Minor pentatonic scales do not always have to start on the root of the chord you are playing over. The minor pentatonic scale starting on the fifth of the chord is common on minor seventh chords. Similarly, the minor pentatonic scale starting on the third of the chord is common on major seventh chords. The example below shows the use of a B minor pentatonic scale over an Emi7 chord. The one after that shows the use of an F minor pentatonic scale over a D♭ major seventh chord.

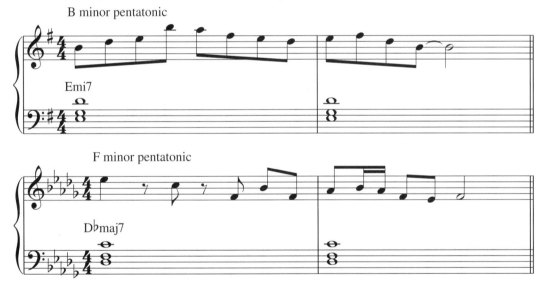

Minor Pentatonic Scale Patterns

The hierarchy among the notes of the pentatonic scale is not as strong as with other scales. While the root of the scale still has a certain gravity to it, and many pentatonic lines start and/or end on the root of the scale, the other notes of the scale are more independent. This is one of the reasons scale patterns sound better and are more widely used with pentatonic scales than with others. The other reason is the fact that pentatonic scales have third intervals in them and not just second intervals like major or minor scales. Therefore, they sound inherently more melodic. In the example below, the same scale pattern is applied to a C minor scale and a C minor pentatonic scale. The pentatonic pattern, while not a genius melody, nevertheless sounds a lot more interesting and melodic than the minor scale pattern.

The etudes that follow introduce a number of pentatonic scale patterns. It is important not only to be familiar with the pentatonic scale in all keys, but to be able to play it using various scale patterns.

Note: The fingerings given for the blues scale and pentatonic scale below are merely suggestions. Unlike the classical major and minor scales, there is no "official" fingering for these scales. The one that works best for you is largely a matter of personal experimentation and preference.

The Harmonic Minor Scale

The Melodic Minor Scale

The Blues Scale in All Keys

(grouped by fingering)

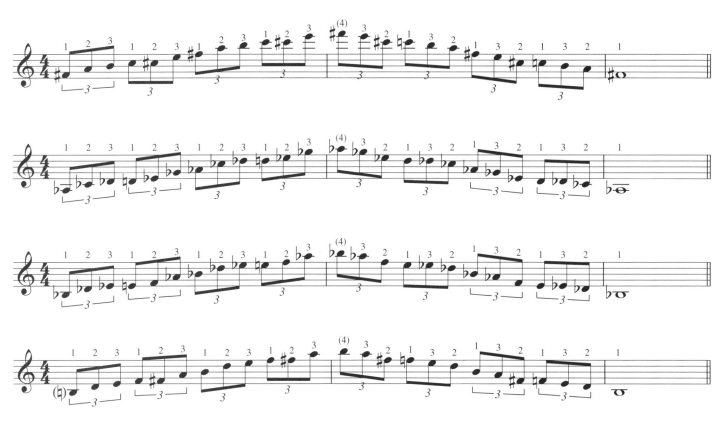

The Minor Pentatonic Scale in All Keys

(grouped by fingering)

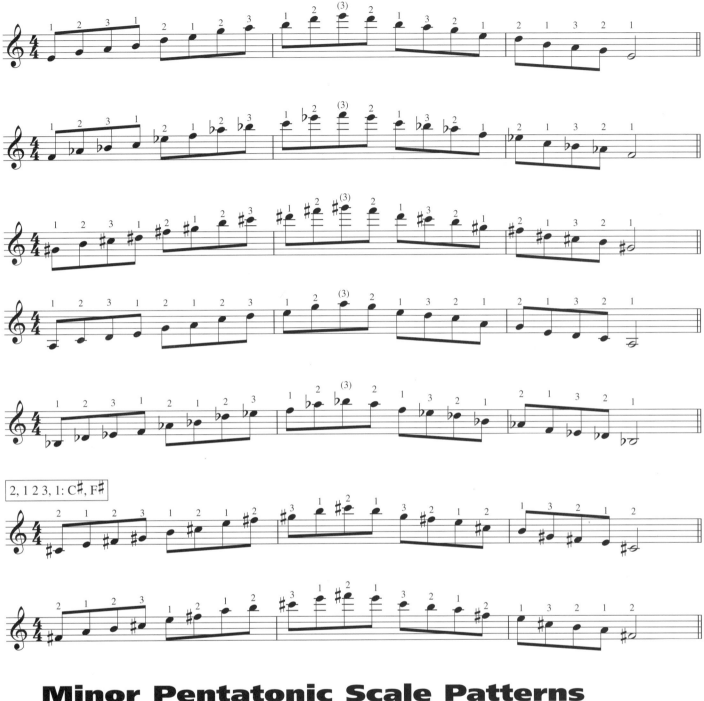

2, 1 2 3, 1: C#, F#

Minor Pentatonic Scale Patterns in All Keys

(practice in all 12 keys)

C minor pentatonic pattern 1: 4-note groupings

C minor pentatonic pattern 2: 3-note groupings

C minor pentatonic pattern 3: 3-note groupings with leaps

Improvisation Concepts

13

First, let's examine the relationship between melody and harmony. As indicated earlier, there are two ways to look at melodies:

- In relation to the key you are in (horizontally)
- In relation to the underlying explicit or implicit harmony (vertically)

The first example shows a purely **vertical** melody. It arpeggiates the underlying chord structures.

The next example shows a **horizontal** melody. The tonic E blues scale is played over a progression of chords. The changing of the underlying chord structures is ignored, melodically speaking.

Sometimes the melodies of songs or sections of songs show either a vertical or a horizontal approach exclusively. Other times, they will mix and overlap.

Vertical versus Horizontal Analysis

The melody notes in both measures of the following example can be analyzed in relation to the key of D major (the key of the song), or the melody notes in measure 1 can be analyzed in relation to the underlying G major triad, and the melody notes in measure 2 can be analyzed in relation to the underlying A dominant seventh chord.

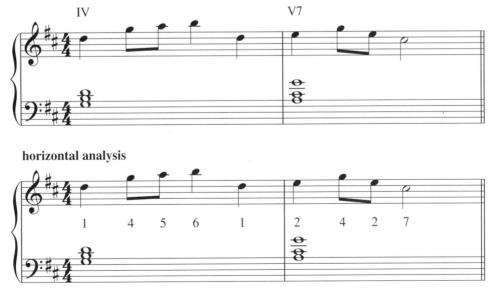

horizontal analysis

vertical analysis

Key-center Improvisation

Key-center improvisation involves lumping two or more chords together, and then playing one scale over them. Usually, this will be a tonic major or minor scale, or a blues scale or pentatonic scale. It is a horizontal approach to improvising. The focus is on one particular scale, usually built on the tonic key of the piece.

Key-center playing makes it relatively easy to solo over a progression, because you have to think about only a single scale, as opposed to using a different scale every time the chord changes. This makes it a good approach for beginning improvisers. Also, using one scale for a whole progression, or a section thereof, automatically creates a certain cohesion.

Key-center playing works best on progressions that are exclusively or predominantly diatonic, or on blues-influenced progressions. The progression below is in the key of A♭ major. All the chords in the progression are diatonic, which makes the A♭ major scale a good choice for improvisation.

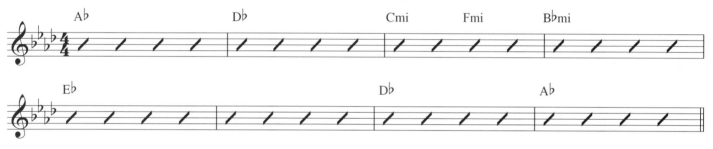

The next example shows a harmonized A♭ major scale. Notice that all the chords from the progression above are contained here:

Chord/Scale Improvisation

The chord/scale approach involves choosing a different scale for each chord and then using those in your solo. It is a vertical approach: The scale always directly corresponds to the underlying chord. You can be specific regarding the notes you play over each chord, a decided advantage. Chord/scale playing also lets you deal with progressions that are too complex for key-center playing.

Chord/scale playing can easily sound mechanical, a decided disadvantage. If you are busy thinking of a new scale every few beats, it is easy to forget that the goal is to play a melody. Complicated scales or instrumental pyrotechnics may impress some people for a while, but accomplished improvisers are ultimately distinguished by their ability to play a good melody.

Chapter 13

While chord/scale improvisation is useful in many different styles of music, it is generally associated with jazz progressions. Some pop songs also contain jazz-like progressions. Typically, they are composed of seventh and extended chords and include a lot of chromaticism. The following example shows a jazz standard progression. The chord/scale approach would work well here.

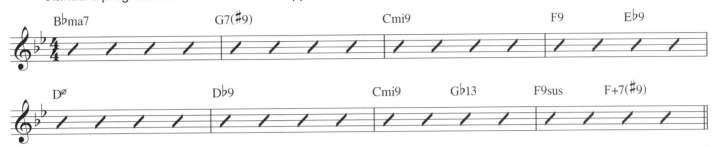

Chord-Shape Improvisation

This approach is built around outlining chord shapes. This usually amounts to the arpeggiating of the underlying chord. This is an excellent method to use when improvising over jazz tunes or progressions with extended chords. It also works well on simple pop songs. The following example shows a four-bar solo over a jazz progression that features predominantly chord shapes.

TRACK 23

In the next example, a tonic D major triad shape (with slight embellishments) is used to solo over a number of diatonic chords in the key of D major:

TRACK 24

Part Five
Practical Application

In Part One, we examined the basics of our diatonic system: major scales, minor scales, and triads. In Parts Two, Three, and Four, we looked at the concepts of harmony, rhythm, and melody. Now, in this last part of the book, we'll look at a number of practical examples to see how all this plays out in "real life."

In **Chapter 14** we'll analyze some comping patterns, in **Chapter 15** we'll look at harmonized scales and how they can be used for both harmonic and melodic purposes, and in **Chapter 16** we'll examine a number of keyboard solos.

Whether you're comping or soloing, the main question is always: How do I create interest? There are two basic ways to do this: **color** and **movement**. Color refers to the vertical coinciding of sounds. For example, adding a ninth to a major triad creates a stronger, more dissonant – and therefore more interesting – color. Playing a blue note like the minor third over a dominant seventh chord that contains a major third creates dissonance as well – in a good way.

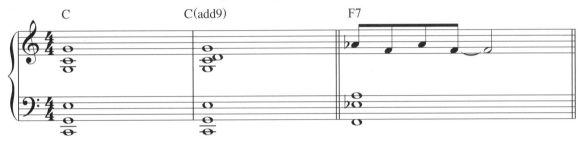

Movement refers to, well, the movement from one thing to another thing. Chord progressions are such movements, as are the juxtapositions of different rhythmic subdivisions or a succession of different melody notes. For example, I could spice up two bars of a C major triad by moving from C to Csus and back to C. I have created movement without leaving the overall harmony, which is C. This is called **elaboration of static harmony**; it is one of the main tools we use to create interest in keyboard playing. Sometimes these movements will be part of the composition, and sometimes we create them spontaneously as we perform.

Bear in mind that you have to operate within the idiomatic parameters of the music you're playing. Throwing eleventh and thirteenth chords into a pop ballad might be just as inappropriate as playing triads on a jazz standard. So yes, you want to be interesting, but not too interesting for the stylistic environment.

Comping Patterns

14

In this chapter, we'll look at a number of ways to spice up your chord accompaniment, whether you're comping behind yourself or somebody else singing – or playing in a band situation.

"Playing time" with your right hand is a great starting point. In the following example, the right hand plays the chords with a quarter-note rhythm. The left hand plays the chord root, as it often does. Rhythmically, it complements the right hand with a couple of syncopated notes. This call-and-response interplay between both hands is very common.

TRACK 25

Whenever there is no bass player (as in solo piano playing or accompanying a singer), the left hand usually plays some kind of bass line. A common approach is to ask, "What would the bass player do, if there were one?" and then try to play something similar. If there is a bass player, you have to be conscious of what you're doing with your left hand. Sometimes you can still play the chord roots in a low register (especially on ballads), but customarily you want to stay out of the bass player's way. Many of the patterns presented here contain a bass line, but they can be adapted to a band situation by leaving out the left-hand part. Frequently, you will need to cover two different parts, anyway. For example, one hand will play the basic comping part and the other will play a string pad.

In the following example, the bass line moves to the fifth at the end of the bar. The fifth is the most common note, other than the root, used in bass patterns.

TRACK 26

In the next example, backcycling is used on beat 4 to create harmonic movement. The rhythm gets busier as well, to coincide with that point of harmonic interest. Note again the call-and-response relationship between left and right hand.

TRACK 27

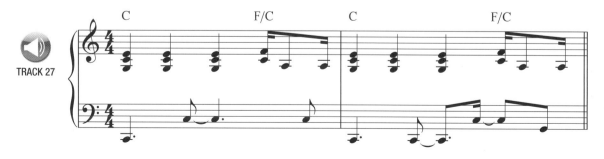

In the example below, moving the top two voices creates interest, while the rest stay the same. This is a form of pedal point. There is an implied harmonic movement that's indicated by the chord symbols, but you could also look at this as two bars of B♭ with embellishments.

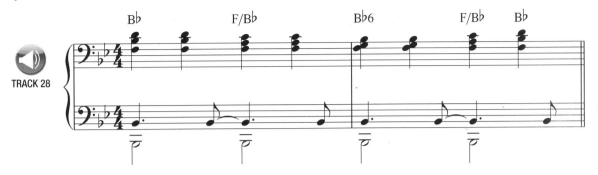

Look at the following chord progression:

Here is a serviceable, if not very interesting, way of playing this:

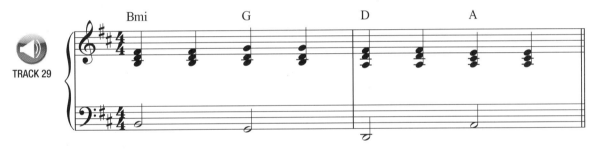

Now, what could we do to spice this up a little? Below is the same two-bar phrase, but with the following transformations applied to it: The B minor chord became a B minor seventh chord, the G major triad became a G suspended chord, and the A chord became a triad with an added fourth. (The latter is a "wrong" chord according to traditional theory, but it is frequently found in pop music.) Notice that the note D is always at the top of the voicing – this is a form of inverted pedal. The left hand plays power chords instead of just roots; this gives more weight to the chords. Now, our two-bar progression sounds a lot more interesting, while still retaining the basic harmonic movement:

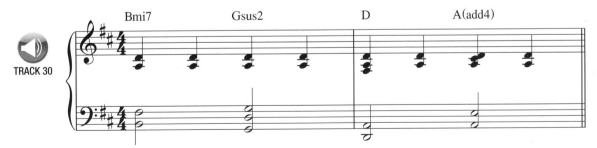

The next example is a four-bar left-hand pattern in the key of F minor. Voice leading is completely ignored in favor of the consistency of the voicing: Each chord is voiced with the root, followed by third and fifth together. The B♭ major chord is a modal interchange chord from the parallel key, F major.

TRACK 31

In the next example, an eighth-note subdivision is used in the right hand. The implied syncopation created by the accents in the right hand is also supported by the syncopated left-hand rhythm. The left hand moves to the flat seven at the end of the bar. That movement from the root down to flat seven and back is encountered time and again in bass lines.

TRACK 32

When using an eighth-note subdivision for the basic rhythmic pattern, it is a regular practice to arpeggiate the chords in some way. The following examples demonstrate a few options:

TRACK 33

TRACK 34

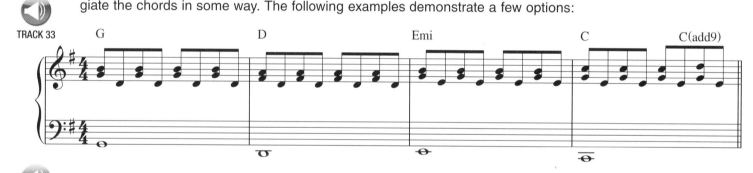

TRACK 35

TRACK 36

In the following example, the grouping of notes in the right hand creates implied syncopation, supported by the syncopated left-hand rhythm:

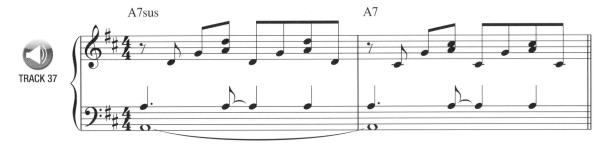

TRACK 37

Employing a 16th-note subdivision for the basic pattern is another well-known option. These patterns are usually arpeggiated. Here are a couple of examples:

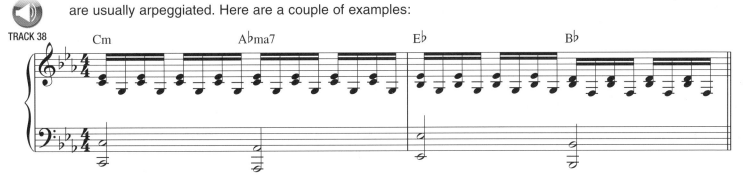

TRACK 38

In the following example, note the melody fragments at the end of the first three bars:

TRACK 39

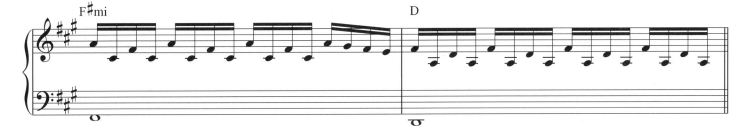

Sometimes, half notes are all you need to get the job done:

TRACK 40

Or dotted half notes. And quarter notes. And dotted quarter notes. And little fills in between them:

TRACK 41

The following examples show how syncopation and suspensions can be used to create interest. Here is a simple way to play a chord progression of B for one bar, and A for one bar:

TRACK 42

Here is the same pattern, but beat 3 is pushed in each bar:

TRACK 43

Now we'll introduce additional harmonic movement by playing a suspended chord first in each bar, and then resolving to the regular triad. The voicing has also changed in order to have the moving voice at the top (the fourth of the chord resolving to the third). The fifth of each chord has moved to the left hand:

TRACK 44

Finally, let's add a little fill at the end of bar one to create additional melodic movement:

TRACK 45

Accenting beats 1 and 2+ is a popular rhythmic pattern. Here are two more examples of this:

TRACK 46

Notice the harmonic complexity in the next example. Slash chords, seventh chords, and add9 chords are used to create interesting colors:

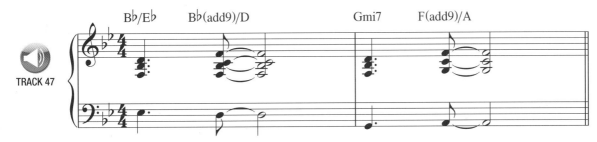

TRACK 47

In the following pattern, alternating between triads, dyads, and single notes creates interest. There's also some syncopation and some melodic fills:

TRACK 48

Next we have two patterns in 6/8. This first one is rather straightforward: The right hand arpeggiates the chords using the basic eighth-note subdivision.

TRACK 49

In the next example, there is a lot of syncopation and call-and-response interplay between the hands. An inverted pedal is created by keeping the note F at the top of the voicing:

TRACK 50

In the following example, the arpeggio is distributed between both hands. The right hand also contains a strong melodic element. This is something you might play as an intro to a pop ballad:

TRACK 51

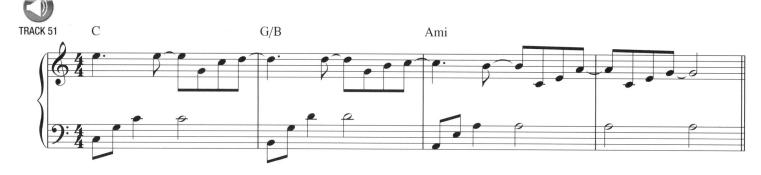

In our final example, the constant rhythmic anticipation creates a flowing rhythm with a strong forward momentum. The chord symbols are an approximation; the notes in the right hand alternately affirm and contradict the implied harmony:

TRACK 52

Harmonized Scales

15

Harmonizing scales is a very common and useful technique in improvising solos or accompaniment patterns. It means to put a chord underneath every note of a scale, using only notes from the scale, and then using the result in a melodic fashion. The following example shows a C major scale, harmonized with root-position triads:

The next example shows a short melodic motif derived from the C major scale, first by itself, and then harmonized with triads:

A scale can be harmonized with root-position chords or inverted chords. Here is a C major scale, harmonized with first- and second-inversion triads:

first-inversion triads

second-inversion triads

A scale can be harmonized with dyads (a chord made up of two notes), triads, or seventh chords. The next example shows a C major scale, harmonized with sixths:

Here is a C major scale, harmonized with seventh chords:

While this technique can be applied to any scale, in popular music it is most commonly applied to the Mixolydian mode. Also, the pentatonic scale harmonized with dyads is an excellent source of material in the creation of funky comping patterns. In jazz, a variety of different scales are routinely harmonized. Gospel music is another style that is full of harmonized scales.

Generally speaking, inverted chords sound much better than root-position chords in the context of harmonized melodies.

Grace notes and chromatic passing tones are frequently used to spice up harmonized scales. The example below shows a C Mixolydian scale, harmonized with dyads. Grace notes are included to give it a bluesy feel.

The Harmonized Mixolydian Scale

The harmonized Mixolydian scale is used frequently, both in soloing and comping. It creates a blues or gospel feel, especially when grace notes are added.

Here is a G Mixolydian scale, harmonized with second-inversion triads:

TRACK 53

The following is a comping pattern using chords from that scale:

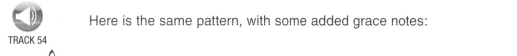

TRACK 54

Here is the same pattern, with some added grace notes:

The Vmi–VImi Technique

The harmonized Mixolydian scale contains minor triads on the fifths and sixths degrees of the scale.

These two triads are often used to create melodies or comping patterns. With the exception of the fourth degree, you can harmonize every note of the Mixolydian scale with either Vmi or VImi.

Note that in this context, first- and second-inversion triads sound much better – and therefore are much more pervasive – than root-position triads. A common variation of this technique involves the interjection of a chromatic passing chord between VImi and Vmi.

The Harmonized Minor Pentatonic Scale

The minor pentatonic scale harmonized with dyads is an excellent source of material for funky comping patterns. Here is a C minor pentatonic scale, harmonized with dyads:

The next example is a funk pattern based on the harmonized C minor pentatonic scale:

Melodies or comping patterns derived from the minor pentatonic scale harmonized with dyads sound good on electro-mechanical instruments such as electric piano, organ, and clavinet. Due to their tonal characteristics, thick, clustery playing that sounds great on acoustic piano is not always the best choice for those instruments.

The I–II–III Technique

Moving from a tonic chord up two steps and/or the other way around is another useful trick. It works well with several different scales.

Below, this technique is applied to the C major scale. Notice that open-position seventh chords are used:

In the next example, the same melody is harmonized, but this time with close-position voicings:

In the example below, the technique is applied to the C Dorian scale. Again, open-position seventh chords are used:

Although the chords in the example below are not technically derived from one particular scale, the pattern is also based on the idea of moving up the scale two steps from a tonic chord. This particular example will work well in a Mixolydian/blues/gospel context. The tonic chord is G, the second one is Ami, and the third chord is B♭. The B♭ chord introduces the minor third relative to the root (G). That, in combination with the major third (B) in the G chord, creates a blues connotation. Also, notice that only inverted triads are used, not root-position triads.

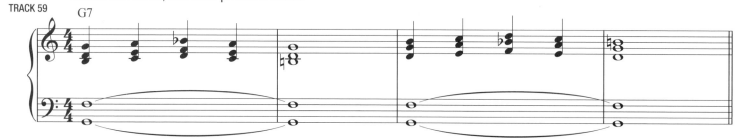

In the next example, a second blue note is introduced by replacing the B♭ major triad with a B♭ minor triad. Both the minor third and the diminished fifth (relative to the tonic, G) are now present. This adds even more bite.

TRACK 60

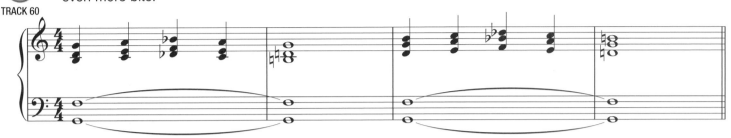

Backcycling

Backcycling is a technique that's closely related to the harmonizing of scales. It involves the creation of harmonic movement by moving backward on the Cycle of Fifths by up to three steps. For example, starting on a C major triad, you can move to the next chord to the left (backward on the cycle), which is F. You can then move on to B♭ and even E♭. All these chords are usually played while pedaling the tonic in the bass, in this case the note C.

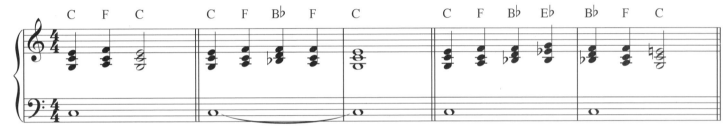

Here are a few rhythmic patterns using this technique:

TRACK 61

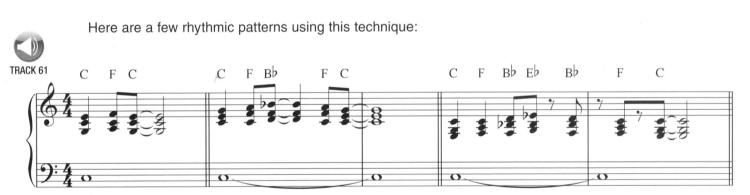

This technique is ubiquitous in every style of contemporary music, especially if only one step is used, as in C-F-C. You can find it all over the playing of singer/songwriters such as Elton John or Billy Joel.

The well-known blues pattern in the next example is another example of backcycling:

TRACK 62

Funk Solo

16

The following (page 112) is a 16-bar solo over a funk groove. The key is F minor and the chord progression is a four-bar harmonic phrase that repeats three times. It contains minor seventh chords on the first, fourth, and fifth degrees of the scale, which suggests a minor blues progression, although this song is not technically a blues. This solo should be played with a Rhodes sound.

From a structural perspective, the solo clearly delineates the four-bar harmonic phrases. When soloing over repetitive progressions like this, it is important to structure your solo in a way that coincides to a certain extent with one-bar, two-bar, four-bar, and eight-bar phrases. This is even truer when there is only one chord to solo over. Of course you don't want to be too obvious about it, either. Pickups or notes at the end of a phrase hanging over into the next bar are ways of avoiding too much predictability.

Melodically, most of the solo is comprised of the F blues scale. This is a classic case of key-center playing. Rather than playing a different scale over each of the three chords, the tonic blues scale is used over all of them. There is only one note in the entire solo that is not derived from the blues scale, and that is G, the second degree of the F minor scale. The G happens either on the Fmi7 chord, as an upper neighbor tone from F (F-G-F), as a passing tone between F and A♭ (F-G-A♭), or on the Cmi7 chord. It is significant that the G is never played on the B♭mi7 chord. It would be the sixth of the chord, and on minor seventh chords you generally don't want to use the sixth a lot, especially if you are not playing a jazz tune.

When analyzing solos, it's a good idea to ask: What happens melodically at the point where the chord changes? In this solo, the root is played six times at the beginning of the bar. The fifth is played four times at the chord change. The third is played three times. This shows that at strategically important points of the solo, you find mostly chord tones, with the root being the most common, followed by the fifth and the third.

In **bar 1**, the melody starts on the root. It moves to the lower neighbor, E♭, and then back to the root. After that, the melody moves to the third via the passing tone, G. It then moves back to the tonic at the beginning of the next bar.

Bar 2 starts with the root of the key (F) played twice. That F is the fifth of the underlying chord, B♭mi7. In the second half of the bar, we have the tonic blues scale. The line begins with the root leaping down to the fifth, and then moves up the F blues scale. Note that the whole bar contains only the tonic blues scale, and doesn't specifically reference the underlying IVmi7 chord.

In **bar 3**, the underlying chord is Cmi7, which is the Vmi7 chord of the key. The melody in this bar is comprised entirely of the blues scale. It moves up and down the scale in a wavelike fashion. The note C is at the beginning of the bar, a subtle but important reference to the underlying chord, Cmi7. Remember that the choice of notes right at a chord change is a crucial element in creating cohesion in a solo.

In **bar 4**, we're back to the tonic minor seventh chord. The melodic line is comprised of the tonic blues scale. It starts and ends on the third (A♭).

Looking at the first four bars of the solo, it becomes clear that, with the exception of one passing tone in bar 1 (the G), the tonic blues scale is used exclusively, in spite of the fact that the chords change every bar. This is classic key-center playing: A single scale is used to solo over a number of chords.

There are several factors that contribute to the overall melodic arc of this four-bar section:

- **The melodic shape.** The line starts out relatively low, and then moves higher up. It reaches its highest point in bar 3 and then gradually moves into a lower range again.

- **The melodic density.** It is at its highest in bar 3.

- **The level of dissonance.** The blues scale is used throughout the four bars. This scale is somewhat dissonant relative to the Imi7 chord, more dissonant relative to the IVmi7 chord, and the most dissonant relative to the Vmi7 chord. In other words, dissonance gradually increases, peaks in bar 3, and then decreases again. It is a fundamental principle in music (regardless of style) that the point in a progression with the greatest melodic, harmonic, or rhythmic dissonance is usually the V chord.

Most well-written music follows the same classic story arc as every other time-bound art form. The way a movie unfolds, builds up to a climax, and then rings out is analogous to the way a piece of music unfolds over time. The four-bar phrase below has that same story arc:

In **bar 5**, the melody is comprised of an F minor triad and one passing tone (B♭). You can also look at it as a five-note position from F to C. Including the grace note (B), they're also the first five notes of the F blues scale.

In **bar 6**, we have more of the tonic blues scale. There is a descending line, starting and ending on B♭, the root of the underlying chord. Notice that there is only one note difference between the F and the B♭ blues scales as applied to this lick. The example below first shows the line from bar 6 of the solo, and then the same line as it would be if it were derived from the B♭ blues scale. Again, the difference is subtle but important. We're in the key of F minor; that's why the first version (the one derived from the F blues scale) is used. The key of the song (F) overrules the chord at that particular moment (B♭mi7).

In **bar 7**, the melody oscillates back and forth between G and E♭, the fifth and third of the underlying Cmi7 chord. This is the only bar in the entire solo where the melody has no obvious relation to the F blues scale or the F minor triad. The chord shape approach is used here.

In **bar 8**, the melody spells out a descending F minor triad with two passing tones. It starts on the third (A♭), which moves down to the root via a passing tone (G). A leap down to the fifth (C) follows, and then another passing tone (B♭) connects the fifth to the third. These two melodic fragments (5-4-♭3 and ♭3-2-1) containing passing tones are used frequently.

A pickup leads into **bar 9**, where the motif 5-4-♭3 continues with a triplet rhythm. At the end of the bar, the third moves to its upper neighbor and back (A♭-B♭-A♭).

In **bar 10**, the melody again comprises the five-note position from F to C. However, the first two notes are B♭, marking the chord change with the root of the chord (B♭mi7) as melody notes. Once again, we have a little reference to the underlying chord (the B♭ on beat 1), as well as a reference to the key of the song (the notes 1-♭3-4-5 of the key, plus the F minor triad starting on beat 2).

The first half of **bar 11** contains a five-note position from C to G, clearly referencing the underlying chord, Cmi7. In the second half of the bar, the melody goes back to the F blues scale.

Bar 11 also illustrates one of the most prominent elements of blues soloing. When playing over a V-I progression, it is very common to first reference the V chord melodically; then, while still on the V chord, we switch to the tonic blues scale and finally move to the I chord. In other words, the I chord is melodically anticipated, usually by a bar or less. In our example, the Cmi7 chord in bar 11 moves to the tonic Fmi 7 chord in bar 12. However, the melody references Cmi7 in the first half of bar 11, and the tonic key of F minor in the second half of bar 11, two beats before the chord progression moves to Fmi7.

In **bar 12**, we first have the familiar movement from the root to the third via a passing tone (1-2-♭3) and back (♭3-2-1). After that, the melody moves to the lower fifth via the seventh and back up again (1-♭7-5-5-♭7-1). Moving from the root down to the fifth via the minor seventh is another common melodic fragment in blues soloing.

In **bar 13**, there is a little motif outlining an Fmin7 chord. In the second half of the bar, the motif is repeated with a slight rhythmic variation. Also, notice how highly syncopated this motif is. Syncopation and rhythmic displacement are integral elements of funk playing.

The melody notes in **bar 14** are derived from the tonic blues scale, despite the fact that the underlying chord is B♭mi7. Again, the tonality (F minor) overrules the chord (B♭mi7).

In **bar 15**, the melody is once more comprised of the F blues scale, in this case played over the Vmi7 chord (Cmi7).

In the **last bar** of the solo, the melody outlines an F minor chord with a passing tone (G) between the root and the third.

Mapping Out a Solo

Mapping out a solo can be helpful. It means to create a game plan, to make decisions as to how to approach a particular chord progression. It will typically involve choosing key center, chord shape or chord/scale as the basic approach, or a combination thereof. It can be as simple as playing a single scale over an entire progression and as detailed as choosing a different scale or a particularly important note for each chord.

Let's create a map for the progression in this unit. We can do this by extrapolating from what we've learned by analyzing the solo. Although the solo is 16 bars long, the progression is really only four bars long, and repeats three times. The chords are Imi7–IVmi7–Vmi7–Imi7. Progressions comprised of I, IV, and V chords often connote blues. Since this is a funk tune, treating it as a blues is a good option.

Let's look at all three chords individually.

Fmi7

Several melodic elements are played over the Fmi7 chord:

* The tonic blues scale (F blues scale)

* The Fmi7 arpeggio in second inversion (C-E♭-F-A♭)

* The second degree of the scale (G), played either as a passing tone (F-G-A♭ or A♭-G-F) or as a neighbor tone (F-G-F)

* An F minor triad with an added note (either the second or the fourth)

The following example illustrates all the options for the Fmi7 chord:

B♭mi7

The melodic elements played over the B♭mi7 chord are as follows:

* the tonic blues scale (F blues scale)

* an emphasis on the note B♭ at the beginning of the bar

The following example illustrates the options for the B♭mi7 chord:

F blues scale   emphasis on the root of the chord at the chord change

Cmi7

The melodic elements played over the Cmi7 chord are as follows:

- the tonic blues scale (F blues scale)

- the third and fifth of the Cmi7 chord (the notes E♭ and G)

- the melodic fragment 1-♭3-4-5 relative to the root of the chord (C-E♭-F-G); five-note position from the root of the chord

- an emphasis on the note C at the beginning of the bar

The following example illustrates the options for the Cmi7 chord:

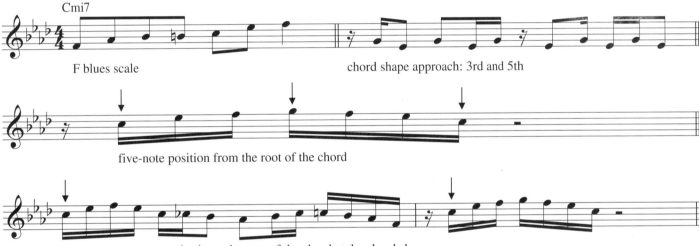

F blues scale   chord shape approach: 3rd and 5th

five-note position from the root of the chord

emphasis on the root of the chord at the chord change

From all the information above, you could create the following simple map for this solo:

- On the Fmi7 chord, play the F blues scale and throw in the occasional G as a passing tone or neighbor tone.

- On the B♭mi7 chord, play the F blues scale with an emphasis on the note B♭ at the beginning of the bar.

- On the Cmi7 chord, play the F blues scale with an emphasis on the note C at the beginning of the bar. Alternatively, play the notes E♭ and G, the third and fifth of the Cmi7 chord, or the melodic fragment 1-♭3-4-5 relative to the Cmi7 chord.

It is even better to go one step further and create the map in general terms, rather than relative to a specific key. This will enable you to play this solo in any key. The non-key-specific map would look like this:

- On the Imi7 chord, play the tonic blues scale and throw in the occasional second scale degree as a passing tone or neighbor tone.

- On the IVmi7 chord, play the tonic blues scale with an emphasis on the root of the IVmi7 chord at the beginning of the bar.

- On the Vmi7 chord, play the tonic blues scale with an emphasis on the root of the Vmi7 chord at the beginning of the bar. Alternatively, play the third and fifth of the Vmi7 chord, or the melodic fragment 1-♭3-4-5 relative to the Vmi7 chord.

This map gives you a framework for your solo, while at the same time leaving enough freedom to be inventive and play new ideas every time you improvise over this tune.

TRACK 63 # Funk Solo

Minor Pentatonic Solo

17

The following is a solo over a IImi7–V7 progression. There are many songs or sections of songs that contain only a IImi7–V7 progression, and the pentatonic scale is a very good choice to improvise over them. Here, the A minor pentatonic scale is used over an Ami7–D7 progression. Notice the use of various scale patterns. Also, since the progression is repetitive and the same scale is used the whole way through, the rhythmic approach is important. Syncopation, 16th-note lines, and triplet figures provide much of the excitement in this solo.

TRACK 64
Pentatonic Solo Over Ami7–D7

Major Scale Solo

18

Now, let's explore various melodic techniques using the major scale. The etude on page 119 is a solo over a four-bar pop progression. Here is the chord progression:

All the chords are diatonic in the key of D major, so key-center playing will most likely be the best way to improvise over the progression. As analysis of the solo will show, the entire solo is diatonic, with the exception of a few grace notes. Furthermore, almost all the notes and phrases can be analyzed in relation to the D major scale or the D major triad, regardless of the underlying chord at any given moment. In other words, despite the fact that the chord progression contains five different chords, the entire solo is an elaboration of two basic concepts: The tonic triad and the tonic major scale.

The example below shows the tonic triad played against the root movement of the chord progression:

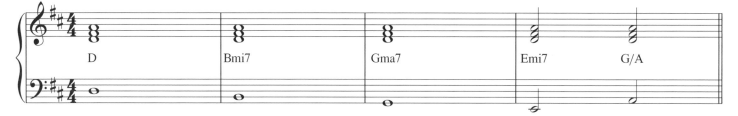

In the following chapters, we will look at various ways of turning these simple elements into interesting melodic material. Some of these concepts overlap; it is often possible to look at the same melody from different perspectives.

Chord Shapes
The Tonic Triad

In the hierarchy of the seven notes of a major scale, the notes of the tonic triad (the first, third, and fifth degrees of the scale) are the most important. Most major scale melodies are anchored around those three notes. Our ears use the tonic note, and by extension the tonic triad, to navigate the tonality of a piece of music. This happens whether we know anything about music or not.

The tonic triad can be used melodically as well as harmonically. The example below shows a D major triad and its inversions used as melodies:

Below, one note of the triad is doubled at the octave to create a four-note chord. Bars 2 and 3 show a famous Mozart melody that uses the chord melodically:

Suspended Shapes

Suspensions are a useful way to create harmonic movement or tension. Likewise, they are often used to create melodic interest. The two most frequently used suspended shapes are sus4 (4 instead of 3) and sus2 (2 instead of 3). The example below shows melodic fragments derived from Dsus4 and Dsus2 chords:

You can find examples of suspended shapes in the following bars of the solo: 5, 6, 7, 9, 10, 13, 14, 20, and 22.

Add9 Shapes

Adding the ninth (or second) to a major or minor triad is ubiquitous in pop music. Again, this works harmonically as well as melodically.

You can find examples of add9 shapes in the following bars of the solo: 5, 6, 7, 9, 10, 11, 12, 13, 17, 18, and 22.

While the vast majority of shapes in this solo reference a D major triad, there is one example of an E minor add9 shape in bar 16.

Add4 Shapes

Adding a perfect fourth to a major triad is somewhat contradictory of traditional theory, but it is not uncommon in pop music. It occurs harmonically as well as melodically. It sounds best with a second-inversion triad.

You can find examples of add4 shapes in the following bars of the solo: 1, 9, 15, 17, and 19.

In bar 10 of the solo, the dominant triad (A major) in second inversion with an added fourth is used over a Bmi7 chord.

Non-harmonic Tones

Non-harmonic tones are a very common way to expand on chord tones. The following can be found in this solo:

Neighbor Tones

A neighbor tone moves away from a chord tone by step and then returns to the same chord tone. The neighbor tones in this solo all reference the tonic triad, D major. Here are the available neighbor tones:

There are numerous examples of neighbor tones in this solo. The following example shows just a few of them:

Passing Tones

A passing tone connects two chord tones. It moves away from a chord tone by step and then resolves to the next available chord tone by step. There can also be two passing tones in a row. The next example shows available passing tones referencing the D major triad:

There are numerous examples of passing tones in this solo. Here are just a few of them:

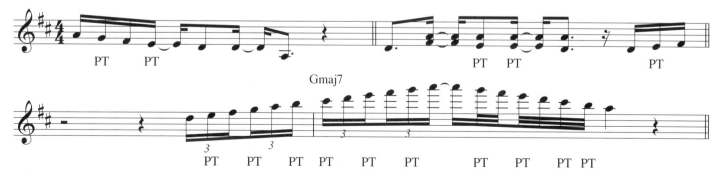

Approach Notes

An approach note precedes a chord tone by a half step or whole step. An approach note is approached by leap, as opposed to neighbor tones or passing tones, which are approached by step. Often, an approach note is the first note of a phrase, in which case it is preceded by a rest. The example below shows possible diatonic approach notes in relation to a D major triad:

Approach notes can be diatonic or chromatic, and there can also be two in a row. Bar 7 of the solo starts out with two approach notes (the grace notes) that resolve to the note F♯. The first approach note is diatonic (E); the second one is chromatic (E♯). There is another approach note on the third 16th note of the bar (the note E, resolving to D). Remember that we are analyzing all the notes in relation to the tonic key, D, and not the underlying chord (in this case Gma7).

Enclosure

An enclosure is a melodic figure whereby a target note is approached by step from both sides. The melodic sequence can be upper approach note/lower approach note/target note, or lower approach note/ upper approach note/target note. Either note can be diatonic or chromatic. More elaborate ornaments are possible with two notes on either side of the target note. (This is common in jazz music.)

Here are several examples of enclosure in relation to a D major triad:

The next example shows an instance of enclosure in bar 21 of the solo:

Hidden Neighbor and Passing Tones

Below is bar 11 of the solo. Although the melodic sequence D–E–F♯ is interrupted by the note A, the note E can still be considered a passing tone, since the A acts more as a rhythmic filler note and not so much as part of the actual melody. This is common. The same note (in this case A) alternating with a melodic sequence (in this case D–E–F♯) can often be ignored for the purpose of melodic analysis.

Pedal Tones

In our solo, pedal tones are ubiquitous. The pedal note is either the root or the fifth of the key. (Those are the notes ordinarily used for pedals.) The following excerpt shows the use of of an upper pedal tone in bars 5 and 6:

Here is a lower pedal tone in bar 21 of the solo:

Bar 22 of the solo contains both an upper and lower pedal tone, with the melody moving in the middle voice:

Positions

Hand positions provide another way of structuring scales. You can lock your hand into a position that spans a certain interval and then work with the available melody notes within that interval. For instance, put your thumb on the root of a scale and your fifth finger on the fifth degree of that scale. (Many exercises for beginning students of the piano are devised that way.) Then, play melodies using all or some of those five notes. We call this a five-note position: 1–5, from the root to the fifth. If you put your thumb on the fifth degree of the key and your fifth finger on the second degree above, we could call this a five-note position, 5–2.

Five-note positions are probably the most common, but others are possible. Four-note positions and octave positions occur quite frequently. In blues playing, these hand positions are standard. Here is a typical octave-position blues lick:

Longer phrases are often stitched together from two or more hand positions. In bar 7 of the solo, the first few notes encompass the five-note position D-A. Then the melody moves lower to a four-note position that encompasses the range from A to D.

Scales

While the entire solo is based on the D major scale, there is only one spot in the solo where regular scalar motion is used. At the end of bar 14, there is an ascending D major scale that continues into bar 15 and then descends back down. You don't usually want to do too much of this, but occasionally it is okay to use scales this way.

Pentatonic Scale

The pentatonic scale is well-used in pop music, as we've already seen. The D major (or B minor) pentatonic scale occurs a few times in this solo.

Major Scale Solo

TRACK 65

Minor Scale Solo

19

On page 122 you'll find a solo over a repetitive Imi–V7–Imi progression in the key of Bb minor. The bass and drums play a Cha-Cha rhythm.

Tonic Chord

On the tonic chord, the melody mostly revolves around the first five notes of the minor scale, thereby avoiding having to choose any particular minor scale (since the different minor scales differ only on the sixth and seventh scale degrees, you can avoid choosing simply by not playing any sixths or sevenths). If I had to choose one, in this case it would be the natural minor scale.

There are a few spots in the solo where other notes are used. The A♮ in bar 9 is a chromatic neighbor tone, and not so much an indication of a harmonic minor scale. Likewise, the Gb in bar 12 functions as a neighbor tone.

In bars 29 through 32, there is a montuno pattern. In bars 31 and 32, the melody moves chromatically from the fifth to the minor sixth to the major sixth, and back. This type of melodic movement is very common is this style.

In bar 36, there is an ascending chromatic line embedded in the triplet figures. It moves from the fifth up to the root, interrupted by rhythmic filler notes on the fifth.

Dominant Chord

The melodic elements used on the F7 chord can be looked at in two ways. From a scale perspective, most notes are derived from the Bb harmonic minor scale.

From a chord shape perspective, most of the melodic content is an elaboration of a dominant flat ninth arpeggio.

Thus, using the chord shape approach to improvisation, the B♭mi–F7 progression can be approached the following way: On the B♭mi chord, anchor your melodies around a B♭ minor triad arpeggio, and then play around it using various melodic techniques (such as passing tones and neighbor tones). On the F7 chord, anchor your melodies around a F7(♭9) chord arpeggio, and then play around it using various melodic techniques (such as passing tones and neighbor tones).

In bars 10 and 11, the chromatic neighbor tone E♮ is used. In bar 14, the chromatic neighbor tone B♮ is used. In bar 34, the chromatic enclosure G♭–E–F is used.

The upper four notes of an F7(♭9) chord form an Adim7 chord; this is called an *upper structure*. The notes of a diminished seventh chords are all minor thirds apart. It is a common melodic device to connect those notes with two chromatic passing tones, as in bars 22 and 23 of the solo.

Chapter 19

Harmonic Minor Scale Solo

TRACK 66

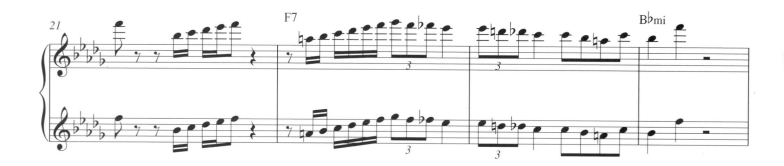

Dance Groove Solos

20

Next, we will analyze two different ways to approach soloing over the following simple four-bar progression.

The drums are playing a medium tempo, four-on-the-floor dance groove.

Although this is a rudimentary chord progression, soloing over it presents its own challenges. You have to answer a number of questions:

- Should I use the key center, chord/scale, or chord shape approach? Or any combination thereof?

- What's the rhythmic feel of my solo going to be? The basic subdivision?

- Should I use single notes? Dyads, triads?

Sometimes these questions can easily be answered by looking at the chord progression or by listening to what the rhythm section is playing. Other times, it is a good idea to try different things and determine what sounds best. As always, some of it also comes down to personal taste.

From a key-center perspective, the chords in this progression are diatonic in a number of different keys: A minor or its relative key, C major; G major or its relative key, E minor. The only difference between the two key centers is that A minor has an F, while G major has an F♯. Interestingly, F versus F♯ is the most difficult question in this solo. The F from the A natural minor scale doesn't sound good on the Ami chord. It sounds too sad, minor-ish. You want a bluesier Dorian sound. The F♯, on the other hand, doesn't sound that great on the G chord. It is too happy, major-sounding. If you look at the example solos, you'll notice that there is only one F♯, and no F♮. In other words, the decision is avoided simply by not playing either note. At any rate, key center is not the best approach for this solo, anyway.

You will find lots of examples of chord shape playing in the two etudes. The trick is to make that sound interesting, since the progression is so simple and repetitive.

From a chord-scale perspective, the A blues or A minor pentatonic scales work best on the Ami chord. They are used in both solos. For the G chord, the G major scale or the G Mixolydian scale could both work, but then you run into the aforementioned problem with F and F♯ again. Both example solos avoid that problem by not using a regular scale at all.

Since this is a dance groove, the rhythmic approach is important. Sixteenth notes make up the basic subdivision. There is lots of syncopation – one of the ways the solos make up for the lack of harmonic interest.

One of the solos contains a lot of dyads. This gives the solo more bite, and also a blues connotation.

The first etude (page 127) is a piano solo over the chord progression mentioned above. The second one (page 128) is a lead synth solo over the same chord progression. It should be played with a monophonic sawtooth lead sound. It makes use of the pitchbend and modulation wheels.

Analysis of the Piano Solo

Let's look at how the two chords in our progression are treated in the piano solo in the first etude.

The melodic material that's played over the **A minor chord** is derived from the A blues scale and the A minor pentatonic scale, respectively.

In bars 1 and 2, a five-note position comprising notes from the A blues scale between A and E is used. The note C♯ at the end of bar 2 is a chromatic passing tone leading to the note D at the beginning of bar 3.

In bars 5 and 6, a long, undulating melodic line is played, again using the A blues scale. Notice the three-note and four-note groupings in the middle of the line. These groupings create irregular rhythmic patterns and are typical of blues and pentatonic playing.

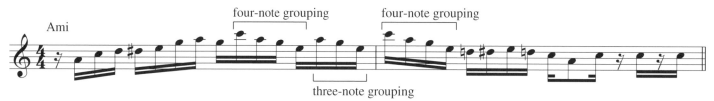

In bars 9 and 10, dyads are used, with an A pedal tone on the top and a bluesy melodic line moving underneath. Again, this is a classic blues lick. Notice the grace notes, the diminished fifth resolving to the perfect fifth.

In bars 13 and 14, we have another blues lick. It contains a dyad C-G (the third and seventh of the Ami7 chord), followed by the note C played as a "shake." A shake is a blues term for tremolo, or trill in classical terms. You "shake" (trill) between the lower C and the G and upper C together.

The notation as 32nd notes is an approximation. The individual notes of a shake don't have to be counted in terms of rhythmic value; you simply trill as fast as you can for the duration of the shake.

Finally, in bars 17 and 18, we have a pentatonic line made up of alternating three-note and four-note groupings. Again, this is classic pentatonic playing. There are only two groupings (D-C-A and E-D-C-A), but because of the rhythmic displacement, the repetition creates a hip melodic effect.

The melodic material that's used on the G major chord is not as easily defined in terms of regular scales. You could put all the melody notes that are used together into a custom scale.

However, it is not practical to use this collection of notes as a scale in the traditional sense. Instead, let's look at some of the melodic combinations used on the G chord in this solo.

In bar 3, we have a G major triad with a chromatic approach note before the B. Minor third to major third – that spells blues. Bar 15 is a variation of this.

In bar 4, there's a lick based on the technique of backcycling. This melodic movement is ubiquitous in contemporary piano playing. It involves moving from the dyad 3-5 to the dyad 4-6 and back, often with the root interspersed. Grace notes are usually added to give it a bluesier flavor. A frequent variation of this lick contains the dyad 5-8.

Bars 4, 7, 8, 11, and 19 are based on this lick. In bar 12, there is a typical blues line consisting of a G major triad whose notes are connected with passing tones.

Analysis of the Synth Solo

Let's look at how the two chords in our progression are treated in the synth solo in the second etude.

Overall, the melodic material is simpler than in the piano solo. There are no blue notes and no dyads. Most lead synth sounds are programmed monophonically, so you could not play more than one note at a time, anyway. Because a synth lead sound is generally much stronger than a piano sound, and because it has such long sustain, you sometimes don't need as many melodic "tricks" to make a solo work as you do when you play piano.

Two elements unique to synth playing are the pitch wheel and the modulation wheel. (On many synths, there is one lever that fulfills both functions.) This solo makes use of both.

The symbol in the music that looks like the roof of a house indicates bending. You play the first note, and then bend up to the second with the pitch wheel or pitch lever. Most synth sounds are programmed so that, from a middle position, you can bend the pitch up or down as much as a whole step. (This is analogous to guitar players, who usually bend notes as much as a whole step.) In the example below, the note G is played, then bent up to A by moving the pitch wheel all the way to the right, or all the way up, depending on the construction on the keyboard you're playing. (This assumes the wheel is programmed to bend by a whole step.) Then the wheel is released back to the starting position, which makes the note return to G.

The trill symbol is used to indicate use of the modulation wheel. Most modulation wheels or levers are programmed to produce some kind of vibrato or tremolo effect. This imitates the effect of, say, a singer or saxophone player bringing in vibrato as they hold a note. The notes are made more expressive.

The melodic material played over the A minor chord is derived exclusively from the A minor pentatonic scale. Notice that the following notes are bent using the pitch wheel:

- The note D up to E and back (bar 3)

- The note G up to A and back (bar 4)

- The note C up to D and back (bars 11 and 12)

- The note C up to D (bar 11)

The modulation wheel is used a number of times to create a vibrato effect on the note A (bars 7, 15, and 16).

The melodic material played over the G major chord consists of a G major triad with two diatonic passing notes, A and C. In other words, we have a G major scale without the sixth and seventh scale degrees.

Digital patterns provide another way to describe the melodic elements. Digital patterns are a sequence of scale steps, usually four to eight notes, which can be applied to different chord qualities:

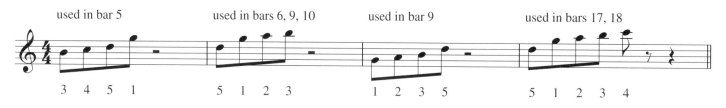

Notice the simplicity of the melody. Interest is created by syncopation, use of the pitch and modulation wheels, and the relatively fast rhythm.

The following notes are bent using the pitch wheel:

- The note A up to B and back, and up to A again, and back, and so on – four times total (bar 6)

- The note A up to B (bar 10)

The modulation wheel is used a number of times to create a vibrato effect on the note D (bars 5 and 9) and on the notes G, A, B, and C in bars 17 and 18.

Dance Groove Solo

TRACK 68 # Dance Groove Synth Lead Solo

R&B Organ Solo

Let's analyze a solo over a blues-related progression, this time with a soul/R&B groove. You can find it on page 135. The chord progression is simple:

The song begins with eight bars of A7, which is clearly the tonic chord. It then moves to the V chord, E7, for two bars. After that, it returns to the tonic chord with a hit on the first beat of the bar, followed by a two-bar break to be filled by the soloist. The chorus concludes with a two-bar syncopated figure that's played four times. Harmonically, this figure is an example of backcycling.

Notice that the key signature is D major, although the tonic chord is A. In blues and related styles, the written key signature often reflects the Mixolydian implication of the I chord (A Mixolydian is derived from the D major scale). Since the note G (the seventh in an A7 chord) is much more likely to occur in this song than the note G♯, the D key signature fits better than an A key signature would.

Bars 1 and 2

Unsurprisingly, the solo starts out with a one-bar lick using the A minor pentatonic scale. The minor pentatonic scale can be used as an alternative to the blues scale – they differ by only one note – and the blues scale is an obvious choice for this tune, since the tonic chord is a dominant seventh chord.

At the end of the lick, the minor third resolves to the major third. Playing a phrase derived from the tonic blues scale or minor pentatonic scale – both of which contain a minor third only – and resolving to the major third at the end of it is a very common melodic device. We've encountered this a lot in previous etudes. The ending of this phrase can also be analyzed as an enclosure of the third.

pentatonic scale resolving to major 3rd   blues scale resolving to major 3rd

The first phrase – and many others in this etude – is quite syncopated. The rhythmic concept of this solo is important. The chord progression is simple, and most of the melodic material is derived from the blues scale, so rhythmic variety is integral to creating enough interest in your improvisation.

first phrase without syncopation   first phrase with syncopation

Bars 3 and 4

The second lick paraphrases the first one. The shape is wavelike instead of descending, and the major third is introduced earlier. It also contains a diminished fifth. (The blues scale is used instead of the pentatonic scale.) Finally, the C# to A interval at the end of the phrase is played twice. Despite these differences, listening to the two phrases back to back confirms that the second one is a response to the first one.

3   ♭5

Bars 5 and 6

The next phrase starts with a two-note pickup into bar 5. The first four notes together spell out an A7 chord, the tonic chord. Notice the dyad A-C#.

A7 chord

The rest of bar 5 and all of bar 6 is another typical example of rhythmic displacement. Repeating a motif that is three 16th notes long in a bar of 4/4, which is normally subdivided into groups of four 16th notes, creates rhythmic excitement. A syncopated rhythm is created by the first note of the motif every time it resets.

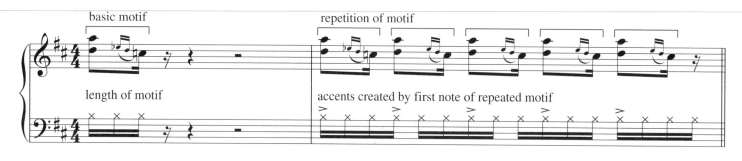

Bars 7 and 8

All the notes in bars 7 and 8 are derived from the A composite blues scale. The first phrase starts out with an A major triad, embellished with two chromatic approach notes: 1) the diminished fifth resolving to the fifth; 2) the minor third resolving to the major third.

The notes in the rest of the bar (starting on beat 2) spell out an Ami7 chord.

In bar 8, we first have the chromatic movement from the third to fifth of the tonic chord, typical of blues, interspersed with two rhythmic filler notes.

The last four notes in bar 8 can be viewed two different ways: 1) 5-6-♭7 relative to the tonic chord; 2) 1-2-♭3 (resolving to 3 in bar 9) relative to the V chord, E7. In the second case, the melody at the end of bar 8 would already anticipate the chord change happening at the beginning of bar 9, a good way to create momentum.

Bars 9 and 10

In bar 9, the chord progression moves to the V chord, E7. It would be possible to play the tonic A blues scale over the V chord. However, since the chord lasts for two full bars, using melodic material relating to the E7 chord sounds more refined. The lick that starts at the beginning of bar 9 and continues through beat 2 of bar 10 should already be familiar: It is an E Mixolydian scale, harmonized with broken sixth intervals. Notice the chromatic passing tones D♯-C.

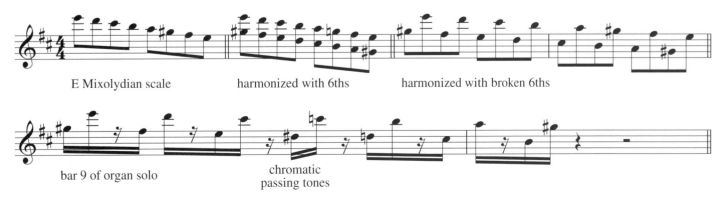

At the end of bar 10, we have the first part of an E composite blues scale.

Bars 11 and 12

In bars 11 and 12, the band lays out. It is common for the soloist to fill a break like that with a busy, often virtuosic, lick. The one presented here is not difficult to play, but it is still quite convincing. It alternates between two triplet motifs, one ascending and one descending, which are repeated throughout the two bars.

Bars 13, 14, 15, and 16

The last four bars of the chorus consist of a one-bar turnaround that's played four times. The turnaround is based on the technique of backcycling (see Chapter 14, page 94), and contains syncopated hits.

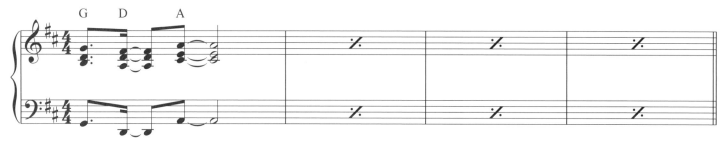

The first half of each bar is busy with the syncopated chord progression, whereas in the second half there is space. The soloist stays out of the way in the first half of each bar (just holding the tonic note, A), and then plays little motifs derived from the submediant blues scale in the second half of each bar, in a sort of call-and-response pattern with the rest of the band.

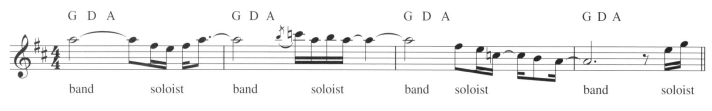

Bars 17 and 18

At the beginning of bar 17, there is a three-note motif starting on A, descending by a whole step and a minor third and then ascending again. The notes fit both the minor pentatonic and the blues scales.

This motif is followed by a sequence of the same motif, meaning that a melody with the same intervallic structure is played, but from a different note of the scale – in this case the fourth, D.

This is followed by a return to the original motif starting on A, which is extended into a longer phrase that includes an enclosure of the notes D and C resolving to the major third, C#.

Bars 19 and 20

This is another example of a motif that is repeated as a sequence. Here are the three variations of the motif:

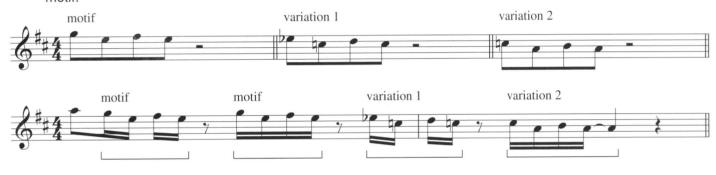

Bars 21 and 22

Bars 21 and 22 contain another lick based on a repeated figure. The notes are derived from the F# blues scale, which is the submediant blues scale relative to the tonic of the chord, A. The four notes used also spell out an A minor sixth chord.

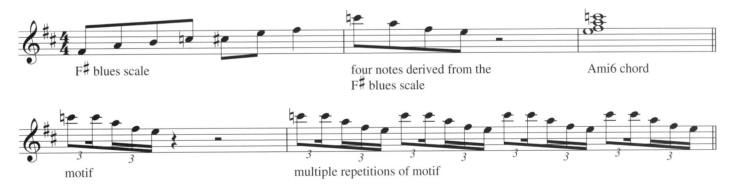

Bars 23 and 24

These two bars contain another lick based on the A composite blues scale. The following melodic elements should be noted:

- Descending chromatic movement from the fifth down to the third, with a small detour via an enclosure of the third.

chromatic movement   enclosure of the 3rd   combination of both
from 5th to 3rd

- Ascending chromatic movement from third to fifth. This happens in bars 23 and 24.

- Chromatic approach note embedded in a tonic triad.

Bars 25 and 26

The first half of bar 25 contains two of the same elements that were just discussed, namely chromatic movement from the third to the fifth and a chromatic approach note embedded in a triad. The only difference here is that it is relative to the E7 chord.

The next part of the phrase contains two chromatic passing tones: one between 8 and ♭7, and one between 6 and 5.

Bar 26 contains the melodic fragment 5-6-8. The triplet figure at the end of the measure already anticipates the return to the tonic chord in bar 27.

Bars 27 and 28

In bars 27 and 28, the band breaks again. The organ lick in these two bars contains familiar material: minor pentatonic and enclosure of the third.

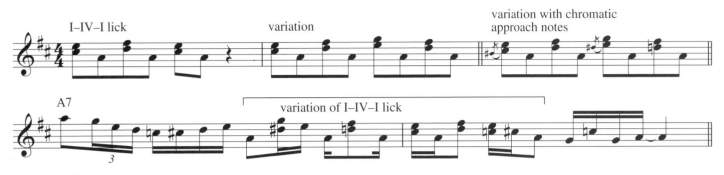

Bars 29, 30, 31, and 32

In these bars, the syncopated turnaround happens again. The solo contains whole notes only, most of them part of a dyad, played with a shake. This is very effective with an organ sound. Often, the player will kick the Leslie speaker effect into high gear at a point like this.

The notes spell out an A minor 11th chord.

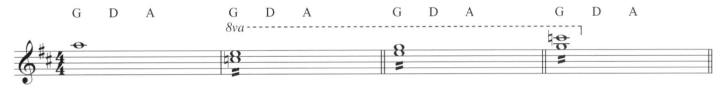

R&B Organ Solo

TRACK 69

R&B Piano Solo

Lastly, we will analyze a piano solo over a 12-bar chord progression made up of nothing but dominant seventh chords. (See page 144.) Though not technically a blues, the progression definitely has a blues flavor. The underlying groove has a slightly funky feel to it. The tempo of this tune is pretty slow, but much of the solo is played with a double-time feel.

A lot of popular music, particularly in rock and R&B, comes straight out of the blues tradition. This solo is a good example of blues playing in the context of popular music.

The solo is based on this progression:

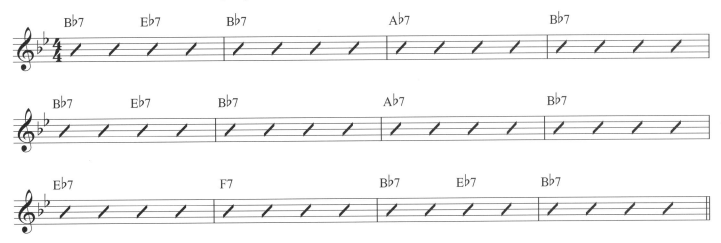

The progression contains dominant seventh chords on the first, fourth, and fifth degrees of the tonic scale, which immediately makes me think "blues." In addition, there is a ♭VII7 chord.

We could use the tonic blues scale to solo over the entire form. The submediant and composite blues scales could be used to add variety. That would be a simple way of handling it. However, in this etude I demonstrate a number of techniques that allow for a more detailed and sophisticated melodic approach. On the following pages, we'll explore those techniques one by one and look at where they are used in the solo. Bear in mind that some of them overlap. In other words, certain melodic elements can be analyzed in more than one way.

The Tonic, Submediant, and Composite Blues Scales

The tonic blues scale, in this case B♭, is a fairly obvious choice for soloing over this progression. It is used extensively here; for example, in the first half of bar 1, and at the end of bar 1 leading into bar 2:

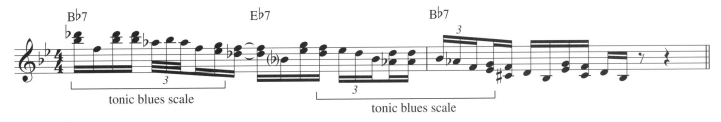

The melody in bars 6 and 7 is derived exclusively from the tonic blues scale:

The lick in bar 16 is another example of the tonic blues scale.

The submediant blues scale is used in bar 19. The chord is A♭7 and the F blues scale is used. F is the submediant of A♭.

The composite blues scale provides a few additional notes as compared to the tonic blues scale: the second, third, and sixth degrees. Here is this scale built on the tonic B♭:

A big portion of the melodic material in this etude can be derived from the B♭ composite blues scale.

Backcycling and That I–IV–I Lick

As we've seen, backcycling is the practice of using neighboring chords on the Cycle of Fifths to create harmonic movement. There is a recurrent melodic device in blues playing related to that technique: the "I–IV–I lick." In its simplest form, it involves moving from a tonic triad to the subdominant triad and back.

There are countless variations of this lick. You can use a different inversion. You can double the root up an octave. You can create rhythmic movement by first playing the two top notes of the triad, followed by the bottom note. You can play each chord twice. The example below demonstrates these variations:

To make it less "major" sounding, add the minor third of the key as a grace note, or as an approach note resolving to the major third.

Playing the minor seventh, instead of the root, at the bottom of the tonic voicing is another standard variation.

The parallel movement of the top two voices (or all three voices) can be extended by another step.

Finally, the I–IV–I lick is often played with a minor triad built on the tonic, instead of the major triad. This creates the juxtaposition of major third and minor third that is so typical of the blues sound. The minor third you're playing in this variation of the lick rubs against the major third you might play in a left-hand voicing, or that might be played by another instrument, or simply implied by the overall context.

The I–IV–I lick and its variations are used in bars 1, 2, 13, and 14 of this etude.

Enclosure and Embellishment of the Third

As previously explained, enclosure is the practice of surrounding a target note with neighbor tones from both sides before resolving. Applying this idea to the third is a very common melodic device in blues playing. In its simplest form, this particular enclosure looks like the example on the following page. Note that the enclosure can be preceded by the third itself, or by any other note, or by a rest. Also, in this context the upper neighbor is almost always played first, followed by the lower neighbor; both neighbor tones are chromatic.

We can interject a whole step below the target note, followed by a half step below – a frequent variation.

There are many variations of this technique. The following example shows a few that are used in this etude:

Harmonized Scales

This etude contains a number of examples of the harmonized Mixolydian scale.

The lick in bar 9 is based on the Vmi–VImi technique, which in turn is derived from the harmonized Mixolydian scale. The underlying chord is E♭7, so the E♭ Mixolydian scale is used as a basis for the melody. Notice the chromatic passing chord on beat 2+.

In bar 10, the same lick is played (with a slight rhythmic variation), but it is a whole step higher to accommodate the underlying F7 chord. This is called melodic sequencing.

The same technique is used in bars 21 and 22. First, there is a lick based on the harmonized E♭ Mixolydian scale, followed by the same lick a whole step higher.

In bar 3, the A♭ Mixolydian scale is harmonized with sixths. The example below shows the harmonized scale first, and then the actual melody. Notice how rhythmic syncopation and the use of grace notes turns this bland scale pattern into an interesting lick.

The lick in the second half of bar 17 takes the same idea even further. Here we have an E♭ Mixolydian scale harmonized with sixths. In addition, chromatic passing notes are interjected.

Positions

Hand positions provide another way to put typical blues phrases together. Refer to previous chapters for an explanation of positions.

Looking at bars 1 and 2 from this perspective, we find the entire lick contains two positions: 1) from the fifth to the minor third; 2) from the root to the major sixth. Each position happens twice, in different octaves.

Now, the space between the top note and bottom note of each position is filled with notes from the blues scale.

The following example shows how each position is turned into a melodic element:

You can see the complete phrase in bars 1 and 2 of the etude.

Chromatic Passing Tones and Chromatic Approach Notes

Chromatic passing tones and approach notes are frequently used to break up the predictability of diatonic scales and to add color to melodies. They are also an important stylistic element of blues playing. Typical examples of chromatic passing tones follow.

- A chromatic passing tone between the major second and the major third of the scale:

- A chromatic passing tone between the root and the minor seventh of the scale:

- Two chromatic passing tones from the major third to the perfect fifth of the scale:

- A chromatic passing tone between the perfect fifth and the major sixth of the scale:

Oftentimes, the chromatic passing tone from the fifth of the tonic chord leads into the third of the subdominant chord:

Chromatic approach notes (abbreviated AN) are preceded by a rest or approached by leap and lead into a chord tone by half-step resolution. The most common of these in blues playing is the minor third resolving to the major third. The diminished fifth resolving to the perfect fifth is also a good choice.

Dyads in Blues Licks

Dyads are customary in blues playing. They provide extra crunch and make the phrases sound fuller. Thirds, fourths, fifths, and sixths sound best. Here are several examples of phrases containing dyads:

Dyads make a phrase more interesting by creating a rhythm within a rhythm. Because the dyads are louder and more dissonant than single notes, they stick out more. The first beat of bar 1 of the solo contains melody notes on every 16th-note beat. Three of them are dyads. This creates an embedded rhythm. The following example shows first the regular rhythm, and then the subordinate rhythm created by the use of the dyads:

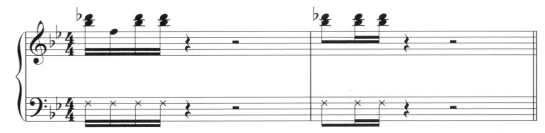

R&B Piano Solo

TRACK 70

KEYBOARD STYLE SERIES

THE COMPLETE GUIDE!

These book/audio packs provide focused lessons that contain valuable how-to insight, essential playing tips, and beneficial information for all players. From comping to soloing, comprehensive treatment is given to each subject. The companion audio features many of the examples in the book performed either solo or with a full band.

BEBOP JAZZ PIANO

by John Valerio

This book provides detailed information for bebop and jazz keyboardists on: chords and voicings, harmony and chord progressions, scales and tonality, common melodic figures and patterns, comping, characteristic tunes, the styles of Bud Powell and Thelonious Monk, and more.

00290535 Book/CD Pack.....................$18.99

BEGINNING ROCK KEYBOARD

by Mark Harrison

This comprehensive book/CD package will teach you the basic skills needed to play beginning rock keyboard. From comping to soloing, you'll learn the theory, the tools, and the techniques used by the pros. The accompanying CD demonstrates most of the music examples in the book.

00311922 Book/CD Pack.....................$14.99

BLUES PIANO

by Mark Harrison

With this book/audio pack, you'll learn the theory, the tools, and even the tricks that the pros use to play the blues. Covers: scales and chords; left-hand patterns; walking bass; endings and turnarounds; right-hand techniques; how to solo with blues scales; crossover licks; and more.

00311007 Book/Online Audio $17.99

BOOGIE-WOOGIE PIANO

by Todd Lowry

From learning the basic chord progressions to inventing your own melodic riffs, you'll learn the theory, tools and techniques used by the genre's best practicioners.

00117067 Book/Online Audio $16.99

BRAZILIAN PIANO

by Robert Willey and Alfredo Cardim

Brazilian Piano teaches elements of some of the most appealing Brazilian musical styles: choro, samba, and bossa nova. It starts with rhythmic training to develop the fundamental groove of Brazilian music.

00311469 Book/CD Pack.....................$19.99

CONTEMPORARY JAZZ PIANO

by Mark Harrison

From comping to soloing, you'll learn the theory, the tools, and the techniques used by the pros. The full band tracks on the CD feature the rhythm section on the left channel and the piano on the right channel, so that you can play along with the band.

00311848 Book/CD Pack.....................$17.99

COUNTRY PIANO

by Mark Harrison

Learn the theory, the tools, and the tricks used by the pros to get that authentic country sound. This book/audio pack covers: scales and chords, walkup and walkdown patterns, comping in traditional and modern country, Nashville "fretted piano" techniques and more.

00311052 Book/Online Audio $19.99

GOSPEL PIANO

by Kurt Cowling

Discover the tools you need to play in a variety of authentic gospel styles, through a study of rhythmic devices, grooves, melodic and harmonic techniques, and formal design. The accompanying audio features over 90 tracks, including piano examples as well as the full gospel band.

00311327 Book/Online Adio $17.99

INTRO TO JAZZ PIANO

by Mark Harrison

From comping to soloing, you'll learn the theory, the tools, and the techniques used by the pros. The accompanying audio demonstrates most of the music examples in the book. The full band tracks feature the rhythm section on the left channel and the piano on the right channel, so that you can play along with the band.

00312088 Book/Online Audio $16.99

JAZZ-BLUES PIANO

by Mark Harrison

This comprehensive book will teach you the basic skills needed to play jazz-blues piano. Topics covered include: scales and chords • harmony and voicings • progressions and comping • melodies and soloing • characteristic stylings.

00311243 Book/Online Audio $17.99

JAZZ-ROCK KEYBOARD

by T. Lavitz

Learn what goes into mixing the power and drive of rock music with the artistic elements of jazz improvisation in this comprehensive book and CD package. This instructional tool delves into scales and modes, and how they can be used with various chord progressions to develop the best in soloing chops.

00290536 Book/CD Pack.....................$17.95

LATIN JAZZ PIANO

by John Valerio

This book is divided into three sections. The first covers Afro-Cuban (Afro-Caribbean) jazz, the second section deals with Brazilian influenced jazz – Bossa Nova and Samba, and the third contains lead sheets of the tunes and instructions for the play-along CD.

00311345 Book/CD Pack.....................$17.99

MODERN POP KEYBOARD

by Mark Harrison

From chordal comping to arpeggios and ostinatos, from grand piano to synth pads, you'll learn the theory, the tools, and the techniques used by the pros. The online audio demonstrates most of the music examples in the book.

00146596 Book/Online Audio $17.99

NEW AGE PIANO

by Todd Lowry

From melodic development to chord progressions to left-hand accompaniment patterns, you'll learn the theory, the tools and the techniques used by the pros. The accompanying 96-track CD demonstrates most of the music examples in the book.

00117322 Book/CD Pack.....................$16.99

POST-BOP JAZZ PIANO

by John Valerio

This book/CD pack will teach you the basic skills needed to play post-bop jazz piano. Learn the theory, the tools, and the tricks used by the pros to play in the style of Bill Evans, Thelonious Monk, Herbie Hancock, McCoy Tyner, Chick Corea and others. Topics covered include: chord voicings, scales and tonality, modality, and more.

00311005 Book/CD Pack.....................$17.95

PROGRESSIVE ROCK KEYBOARD

by Dan Maske

You'll learn how soloing techniques, form, rhythmic and metrical devices, harmony, and counterpoint all come together to make this style of rock the unique and exciting genre it is.

00311307 Book/CD Pack.....................$17.95

R&B KEYBOARD

by Mark Harrison

From soul to funk to disco to pop, you'll learn the theory, the tools, and the tricks used by the pros with this book/CD pack. Topics covered include: scales and chords, harmony and voicings, progressions and comping, rhythmic concepts, characteristic stylings, the development of R&B, and more! Includes seven songs.

00310881 Book/CD Pack.....................$17.95

ROCK KEYBOARD

by Scott Miller

Learn to comp or solo in any of your favorite rock styles. Listen to the audio to hear your parts fit in with the total groove of the band. Includes 99 tracks! Covers: classic rock, pop/rock, blues rock, Southern rock, hard rock, progressive rock, alternative rock and heavy metal.

00310823 Book/Online Audio $17.95

ROCK 'N' ROLL PIANO

by Andy Vinter

Take your place alongside Fats Domino, Jerry Lee Lewis, Little Richard, and other legendary players of the '50s and '60s! This book/CD pack covers: left-hand patterns; basic rock 'n' roll progressions; right-hand techniques; straight eighths vs. swing eighths; glisses, crushed notes, rolls, note clusters and more. Includes six complete tunes.

00310912 Book/CD Pack.....................$17.99

SALSA PIANO

by Hector Martignon

From traditional Cuban music to the more modern Puerto Rican and New York styles, you'll learn the all-important rhythmic patterns of salsa and how to apply them to the piano. The book provides historical, geographical and cultural background info, and the 50+-track CD includes piano examples and a full salsa band percussion section.

00311049 Book/CD Pack.....................$17.95

SMOOTH JAZZ PIANO

by Mark Harrison

Learn the skills you need to play smooth jazz piano – the theory, the tools, and the tricks used by the pros. Topics covered include: scales and chords; harmony and voicings; progressions and comping; rhythmic concepts; melodies and soloing; characteristic stylings; discussions on jazz evolution.

00311095 Book/CD Pack.....................$17.95

STRIDE & SWING PIANO

by John Valerio

Learn the styles of the stride and swing piano masters, such as Scott Joplin, Jimmy Yancey, Pete Johnson, Jelly Roll Morton, James P. Johnson, Fats Waller, Teddy Wilson, and Art Tatum. This book/CD pack covers classic ragtime, early blues and boogie woogie, New Orleans jazz and more. Includes 14 songs.

00310882 Book/CD Pack.....................$17.95

Prices, contents, and availability
subject to change without notice.

www.halleonard.com

7777 W. BLUEMOUND RD. P.O. BOX 13819 MILWAUKEE, WI 53213

0416